C000065247

Teacher's Guide 2

Vocabulary, Grammar and Punctuation Skills

Author: Abigail Steel

William Collins' dream of knowledge for all began with the publication of his first book in 1819.

A self-educated mill worker, he not only enriched millions of lives, but also founded a flourishing publishing house. Today, staying true to this spirit, Collins books are packed with inspiration, innovation and practical expertise. They place you at the centre of a world of possibility and give you exactly what you need to explore it.

Collins. Freedom to teach.

An imprint of HarperCollins*Publishers*
The News Building
1 London Bridge Street
London
SE1 9GF

Browse the complete Collins catalogue at
www.collins.co.uk

British Library Cataloguing in Publication Data

A catalogue record for this publication is available from the British Library.

Publishing Director: Lee Newman
Publishing Manager: Helen Doran
Senior Editor: Hannah Dove
Project Manager: Emily Hooton
Author: Abigail Steel
Development Editor: Jessica Marshall
Copy-editor: Karen Williams
Proofreader: Gaynor Spry
Cover design and artwork: Amparo Barrera and Ken Vail Graphic Design
Internal design concept: Amparo Barrera
Typesetter: Ken Vail Graphic Design
Illustrations: Alberto Saichann (Beehive Illustration)
Production Controller: Rachel Weaver

Printed and bound by CPI Group (UK) Ltd, Croydon, CR0 4YY

Contents

About Treasure House

Treasure House is a comprehensive and flexible bank of books and online resources for teaching the English curriculum. The Treasure House series offers two different pathways: one covering each English strand discretely (Skills Focus Pathway) and one integrating texts and the strands to create a programme of study (Integrated English Pathway). This Teacher's Guide is part of the Skills Focus Pathway.

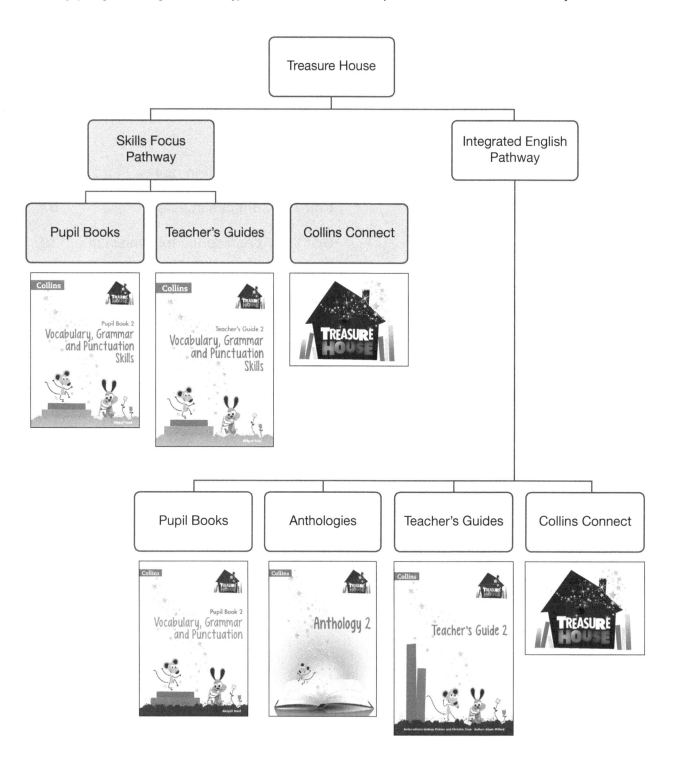

1. Skills Focus

The Skills Focus Pupil Books and Teacher's Guides for all four strands (Comprehension; Spelling; Composition; and Vocabulary, Grammar and Punctuation) allow you to teach each curriculum area in a targeted way. Each unit in the Pupil Book is mapped directly to the statutory requirements of the National Curriculum. Each Teacher's Guide provides step-by-step instructions to guide you through the Pupil Book activities and digital Collins Connect resources for each competency. With a clear focus on skills and clearly-listed curriculum objectives you can select the appropriate resources to support your lessons.

  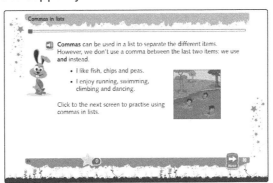

2. Integrated English

Alternatively, the Integrated English pathway offers a complete programme of genre-based teaching sequences. There is one Teacher's Guide and one Anthology for each year group. Each Teacher's Guide provides 15 teaching sequences focused on different genres of text such as fairy tales, letters and newspaper articles. The Anthologies contain the classic texts, fiction, non-fiction and poetry required for each sequence. Each sequence also weaves together all four dimensions of the National Curriculum for English – Comprehension; Spelling; Composition; and Vocabulary, Grammar and Punctuation – into a complete English programme. The Pupil Books and Collins Connect provide targeted explanation of key points and practice activities organised by strand. This programme provides 30 weeks of teaching inspiration.

Other components

Handwriting Books, Handwriting Workbooks, Word Books and the online digital resources on Collins Connect are suitable for use with both pathways.

  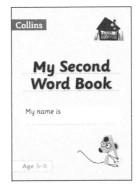

Treasure House Skills Focus Teacher's Guides

Year	Comprehension	Composition	Vocabulary, Grammar and Punctuation	Spelling
1	978-0-00-822290-1	978-0-00-822302-1	978-0-00-822296-3	978-0-00-822308-3
2	978-0-00-822291-8	978-0-00-822303-8	978-0-00-822297-0	978-0-00-822309-0
3	978-0-00-822292-5	978-0-00-822304-5	978-0-00-822298-7	978-0-00-822310-6
4	978-0-00-822293-2	978-0-00-822305-2	978-0-00-822299-4	978-0-00-822311-3
5	978-0-00-822294-9	978-0-00-822306-9	978-0-00-822300-7	978-0-00-822312-0
6	978-0-00-822295-6	978-0-00-822307-6	978-0-00-822301-4	978-0-00-822313-7

Inside the Skills Focus Teacher's Guides

The teaching notes in each unit in the Teacher's Guide provide you with subject information or background, a range of whole class and differentiated activities including photocopiable resource sheets and links to the Pupil Book and the online Collins Connect activities.

Each **Overview** provides clear objectives for each lesson tied into the new curriculum, links to the other relevant components and a list of any additional resources required.

Teaching overview provides a brief introduction to the specific concept or rule and some pointers on how to approach it.

Support, embed & challenge supports a mastery approach with activities provided at three levels.

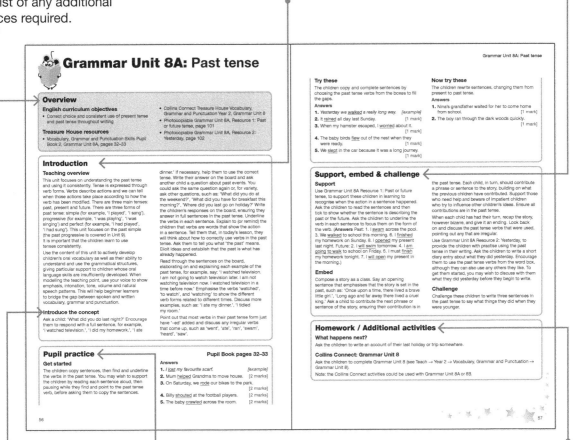

Introduce the concept provides 5–10 minutes of preliminary discussion points or class/group activities to get the pupils engaged in the lesson focus and set out any essential prior learning.

Pupil practice gives guidance and the answers to each of the three sections in the Pupil Book: *Get started*, *Try these* and *Now try these*.

Homework / Additional activities lists ideas for classroom or homework activities, and relevant activities from Collins Connect.

Two photocopiable **resource** worksheets per unit provide extra practice of the specific lesson concept. They are designed to be used with the activities in support, embed or challenge sections.

Treasure House Skills Focus Pupil Books

There are four Skills Focus Pupil Books for each year group, based on the four dimensions of the National Curriculum for English: Comprehension; Spelling; Composition; and Vocabulary, Grammar and Punctuation. The Pupil Books provide a child-friendly introduction to each subject and a range of initial activities for independent pupil-led learning. A Review unit for each term assesses pupils' progress.

Year	Comprehension	Composition	Vocabulary, Grammar and Punctuation	Spelling
1	978-0-00-823634-2	978-0-00-823646-5	978-0-00-823640-3	978-0-00-823652-6
2	978-0-00-823635-9	978-0-00-823647-2	978-0-00-823641-0	978-0-00-823653-3
3	978-0-00-823636-6	978-0-00-823648-9	978-0-00-823642-7	978-0-00-823654-0
4	978-0-00-823637-3	978-0-00-823649-6	978-0-00-823643-4	978-0-00-823655-7
5	978-0-00-823638-0	978-0-00-823650-2	978-0-00-823644-1	978-0-00-823656-4
6	978-0-00-823639-7	978-0-00-823651-9	978-0-00-823645-8	978-0-00-823657-1

Inside the Skills Focus Pupil Books

Comprehension

Includes high-quality text extracts covering poetry, prose, traditional tales, playscripts and non-fiction.

Pupils retrieve and record information, learn to draw inferences from texts and increase their familiarity with a wide range of literary genres.

Composition

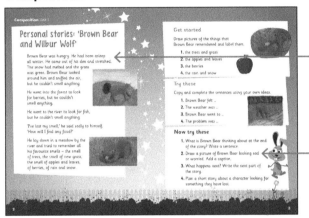

Includes high-quality, annotated text extracts as models for different types of writing.

Children learn how to write effectively and for a purpose.

Vocabulary, Grammar and Punctuation

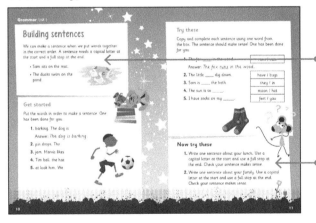

Develops children's knowledge and understanding of grammar and punctuation skills.

A rule is introduced and explained. Children are given lots of opportunities to practise using it.

Spelling

Spelling rules are introduced and explained.

Practice is provided for spotting and using the spelling rules, correcting misspelt words and using the words in context.

Treasure House on Collins Connect

Digital resources for Treasure House are available on Collins Connect which provides a wealth of interactive activities. Treasure House is organised into six core areas on Collins Connect:

- Comprehension
- Spelling
- Composition
- Vocabulary, Grammar and Punctuation
- The Reading Attic
- Teacher's Guides and Anthologies.

For most units in the Skills Focus Pupil Books, there is an accompanying Collins Connect unit focused on the same teaching objective. These fun, independent activities can be used for initial pupil-led learning, or for further practice using a different learning environment. Either way, with Collins Connect, you have a wealth of questions to help children embed their learning.

Treasure House on Collins Connect is available via subscription at connect.collins.co.uk

Features of Treasure House on Collins Connect

The digital resources enhance children's comprehension, spelling, composition, and vocabulary, grammar, punctuation skills through providing:

- a bank of varied and engaging interactive activities so children can practise their skills independently
- audio support to help children access the texts and activities
- auto-mark functionality so children receive instant feedback and have the opportunity to repeat tasks.

Teachers benefit from useful resources and time-saving tools including:

- teacher-facing materials such as audio and explanations for front-of-class teaching or pupil-led learning
- lesson starter videos for some Composition units
- downloadable teaching notes for all online activities
- downloadable teaching notes for Skills Focus and Integrated English pathways
- the option to assign homework activities to your classes
- class records to monitor progress.

Comprehension

- Includes high-quality text extracts covering poetry, prose, traditional tales, playscripts and non-fiction.
- Audio function supports children to access the text and the activities

Composition

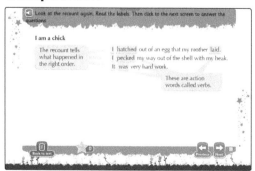

- Activities support children to develop and build more sophisticated sentence structures.
- Every unit ends with a longer piece of writing that can be submitted to the teacher for marking.

Vocabulary, Grammar and Punctuation

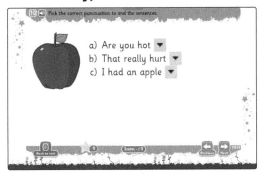

- Fun, practical activities develop children's knowledge and understanding of grammar and punctuation skills.
- Each skill is reinforced with a huge, varied bank of practice questions.

Spelling

- Fun, practical activities develop children's knowledge and understanding of each spelling rule.
- Each rule is reinforced with a huge, varied bank of practice questions.
- Children spell words using an audio prompt, write their own sentences and practise spelling using Look Say Cover Write Check.

Reading Attic

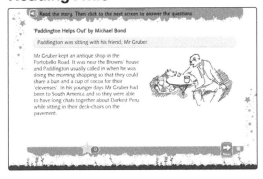

- Children's love of reading is nurtured with texts from exciting children's authors including Micheal Bond, David Walliams and Micheal Morpurgo.
- Lesson sequences accompany the texts, with drama opportunities and creative strategies for engaging children with key themes, characters and plots.
- Whole-book projects encourage reading for pleasure.

Treasure House Digital Teacher's Guides and Anthologies

The teaching sequences and anthology texts for each year group are included as a flexible bank of resources.

The teaching notes for each skill strand and year group are also included on Collins Connect.

Support, embed and challenge

Treasure House provides comprehensive, detailed differentiation at three levels to ensure that all children are able to access achievement. It is important that children master the basic skills before they go further in their learning. Children may make progress towards the standard at different speeds, with some not reaching it until the very end of the year.

In the Teacher's Guide, Support, Embed and Challenge sections allow teachers to keep the whole class focussed with no child left behind. Two photocopiable resources per unit offer additional material linked to the Support, Embed or Challenge sections.

Support

The Support section offers simpler or more scaffolded activities that will help learners who have not yet grasped specific concepts covered. Background information may also be provided to help children to contextualise learning. This enables children to make progress so that they can keep up with the class.

In Vocabulary, Grammar and Punctuation Teacher's Guides, the activities in the Support section help children to access the rules by giving additional practice of the key teaching point.

If you have a teaching assistant, you may wish to ask him or her to help children work through these activities. You might then ask children who have completed these activities to progress to other more challenging tasks found in the Embed or Challenge sections – or you may decide more practice of the basics is required. Collins Connect can provide further activities.

Embed

The Embed section includes activities to embed learning and is aimed at those who children who are working at the expected standard. It ensures that learners have understood key teaching objectives for the age-group. These activities could be used by the whole class or groups, and most are appropriate for both teacher-led and independent work.

For Vocabulary, Grammar and Punctuation, the activities in Embed enhance children's understanding by offering additional opportunities for the rules to be applied in a variety of contexts.

Challenge

The Challenge section provides additional tasks, questions or activities that will push children who have mastered the concept without difficulty. This keeps children motivated and allows them to gain a greater depth of understanding. You may wish to give these activities to fast finishers to work through independently.

In Vocabulary, Grammar and Punctuation, the challenge activities offer children with the opportunity to work at a higher level by extending the investigation and application of rules to a wider variety of different contexts.

Assessment

Teacher's Guides

There are opportunities for assessment throughout the Treasure House series. The teaching notes in Treasure House Teacher's Guides offer ideas for questions, informal assessment and spelling tests.

Pupil Book Review units

Each Pupil Book has three Review units designed as a quick formative assessment tool for the end of each term. Questions assess the work that has been covered over the previous units. These review units will provide you with an informal way of measuring your pupils' progress. You may wish to use these as Assessment for Learning to help you and your pupils to understand where they are in their learning journey.

The Review units in the Vocabulary, Grammar and Punctuation Pupil Books, include questions testing rules taught in preceding units. By mixing questions on different unit topics within exercises, children can show understanding of multiple rules and patterns.

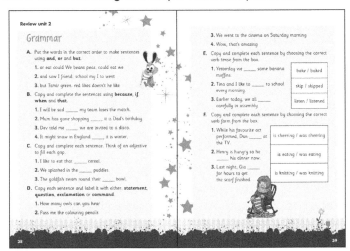

Assessment in Collins Connect

Activities on Collins Connect can also be used for effective assessment. Activities with auto-marking mean that if children answer incorrectly, they can make another attempt helping them to analyse their own work for mistakes. Homework activities can also be assigned to classes through Collins Connect. At the end of activities, children can select a smiley face to indicate how they found the task giving you useful feedback on any gaps in knowledge.

Class records on Collins Connect allow you to get an overview of children's progress with several features. You can choose to view records by unit, pupil or strand. By viewing detailed scores, you can view pupils' scores question by question in a clear table-format to help you establish areas where there might be particular strengths and weaknesses both class-wide and for individuals.

If you wish, you can also set mastery judgements (mastery achieved and exceeded, mastery achieved, mastery not yet achieved) to help see where your children need more help.

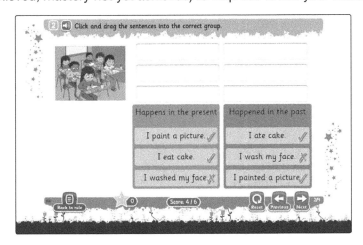

Support with teaching vocabulary, grammar and punctuation

The teacher's guides for Vocabulary, Grammar and Punctuation units can be followed in a simple linear fashion that structures the lesson into four sections:

- assessment of existing skills and knowledge, and an introduction to the unit's teaching point
- completion of the 'pupil practice' questions
- differentiated work, following the Support, Embed and Challenge activity guidance (using the provided photocopiable worksheets)
- homework or additional activities.

However, this lesson structure is intended to be flexible. While we recommend that the first two of these steps should usually be followed in the given order, work following the pupil practice questions can be manipulated in numerous ways to suit the needs, skills and preferences of your class. For example, you may wish to set one of the differentiation activities as homework for the whole class, or to guide children through an 'additional' activity during the lesson, rather than setting it as homework. You may alternatively judge that your class has firmly grasped the concept being taught, and choose not to use any activity suggested, or perhaps introduce only the Extend activity: it is not essential that every activity outlined in the teacher's guide units should be completed.

With the same motivation, many activities (and worksheets) could be adapted for reuse in units other than the one for which they are provided. Several activity and worksheet types are already repeated in similar forms between (and sometimes within) year groups. This is in order both to show the children's changing levels of attainment directly, and to allow any children who have found an activity challenging to reattempt it in a new context after developing their skills.

You may also wish to consider using Support activities in conjunction with the pupil practice questions, if children are struggling with content or a concept with which the Support activity deals. For example, if questions within the 'Try these' and 'Now try these' sections of pupil practice require understanding of adverbials, you may wish to intervene and prepare children using an appropriate Support activity.

By using the teacher's guide units and their suggested activities flexibly, you can choose to tailor the resources at your fingertips to provide the most beneficial learning system for the children being taught. Having confidence in English vocabulary, grammar and punctuation prepares children to function effectively in society as they mature. The aim therefore is to equip children with a strong command of the spoken and written word.

We can make learning vocabulary, grammar and punctuation easy and fun by employing simple techniques to guide children along their literacy journey.

Vocabulary: Establish an ethos in your classroom where words are 'cool'. Talk about your desire to use words that are not the biggest, or the fanciest, or the most complex but that are the 'right words for the job'. Try not to make assumptions about children's level of vocabulary, sometimes those that have a wide vocabulary do not always know the right times to use it. Consider introducing a word of the week, or word of the day. Mention new, unusual or effective words when reading any text in a natural way, for example, say: 'Oh, what a great word I must remember to use that sometime'. Ensure children are so familiar with using dictionaries and thesaurus's that it becomes second nature for them to use them efficiently when reading and writing.

Grammar: Grammar can be tricky to learn and to teach, especially with primary aged children. Explain to them that having a solid working knowledge of grammar enables them to control their spoken and written words in a way that they can influence and affect their reader effectively. Sometimes the very best authors use their knowledge of grammar rules to break them and create interesting effects! Try to make grammar as simple as possible whilst giving enough explanation to be memorable and logical. Repetition is important to help children embed elements of grammar. Another important aspect is demonstrating grammar in real life contexts so children can experience how and why it is needed. A fun activity can be to show the wrong grammar in modeled sentences on the board. This also demonstrates to children how much grammar they have already picked up through their daily use of language, both spoken and written.

Punctuation: Punctuation is generally more straightforward to get to grips with but it does require lots of repetition for children to remember to use it correctly! You can talk to children incidentally about any punctuation marks they come across in wider literature at the same time as focusing on a few aspects at a time through your planned teaching. Model examples of writing with and without punctuation marks to help children notice the different effects.

Delivering the 2014 National Curriculum for English

Unit	Title	Treasure House Resources	Collins Connect	English Programme of Study	KS1 English Grammar, Punctuation and Spelling Test code
Vocabulary					
1	Using suffixes to form nouns	• Vocabulary, Grammar and Punctuation Skills Pupil Book 2, Vocabulary Unit 1, pages 4–5 • Vocabulary, Grammar and Punctuation Skills Teacher's Guide 2 – Vocabulary Unit 1, pages 22–24 – Photocopiable Vocabulary Unit 1, Resource 1: –ness words word search, page 75 – Photocopiable Vocabulary Unit 1, Resource 2: –ness word sentences, page 76	Treasure House Vocabulary, Grammar and Punctuation Year 2, Vocabulary Unit 1	Formation of nouns using suffixes such as '–ness', '–er' and by compounding [for example, 'whiteboard', 'superman']	G8.3
2	Compound nouns	• Vocabulary, Grammar and Punctuation Skills Pupil Book 2, Vocabulary Unit 2, pages 6–7 • Vocabulary, Grammar and Punctuation Skills Teacher's Guide 2 – Vocabulary Unit 2, pages 25–27 – Photocopiable Vocabulary Unit 2, Resource 1: Making compound nouns, page 77 – Photocopiable Vocabulary Unit 2, Resource 2: Compound noun definitions, page 78	Treasure House Vocabulary, Grammar and Punctuation Year 2, Vocabulary Unit 2	Formation of nouns using suffixes such as '–ness', '–er' and by compounding [for example, 'whiteboard', 'superman']	G8.3
3	Using suffixes to form adjectives	• Vocabulary, Grammar and Punctuation Skills Pupil Book 2, Vocabulary Unit 3, pages 8–9 • Vocabulary, Grammar and Punctuation Skills Teacher's Guide 2 – Vocabulary Unit 3, pages 28–29 – Photocopiable Vocabulary Unit 3, Resource 1: –ful and –less words crossword, page 79 – Photocopiable Vocabulary Unit 3, Resource 2: –ful and –less word sentences, page 80	Treasure House Vocabulary, Grammar and Punctuation Year 2, Vocabulary Unit 3	Formation of adjectives using suffixes such as '–ful', '–less'	G8.3

Unit	Title	Treasure House Resources	Collins Connect	English Programme of Study	KS1 English Grammar, Punctuation and Spelling Test code
4	Using suffixes to form adverbs from adjectives	• Vocabulary, Grammar and Punctuation Skills Pupil Book 2, Vocabulary Unit 4, pages 10–11 • Vocabulary, Grammar and Punctuation Skills Teacher's Guide 2 – Vocabulary Unit 4, pages 30–32 – Photocopiable Vocabulary Unit 4, Resource 1: Adverb word sums, page 81 – Photocopiable Vocabulary Unit 4, Resource 2: Sentence building, page 82	Treasure House Vocabulary, Grammar and Punctuation Year 2, Vocabulary Unit 4	Use of the suffixes '–er', '–est' in adjectives and the use of '–ly' in Standard English to turn adjectives into adverbs	G1.6
5	Using suffixes in adjectives	• Vocabulary, Grammar and Punctuation Skills Pupil Book 2, Vocabulary Unit 5, pages 12–13 • Vocabulary, Grammar and Punctuation Skills Teacher's Guide 2 – Vocabulary Unit 5, pages 33–35 – Photocopiable Vocabulary Unit 5, Resource 1: Comparative sentences, page 83 – Photocopiable Vocabulary Unit 5, Resource 2: Comparisons quiz, page 84	Treasure House Vocabulary, Grammar and Punctuation Year 2, Vocabulary Unit 5	Use of the suffixes '–er', '–est' in adjectives and the use of '–ly' in Standard English to turn adjectives into adverbs	G1.6
Grammar					
1	Coordinating conjunctions	• Vocabulary, Grammar and Punctuation Skills Pupil Book 2, Grammar Unit 1, pages 16–17 • Vocabulary, Grammar and Punctuation Skills Teacher's Guide 2 – Grammar Unit 1, pages 37–38 – Photocopiable Grammar Unit 1, Resource 1: Building coordinating conjunction sentences, page 85 – Photocopiable Grammar Unit 1, Resource 2: Finishing coordinating conjunction sentences, page 86	Treasure House Vocabulary, Grammar and Punctuation Year 2, Grammar Unit 1	Subordination (using 'when', 'if', 'that', 'because') and coordination (using 'or', 'and', 'but')	G3.3 G3.4

Unit	Title	Treasure House Resources	Collins Connect	English Programme of Study	KS1 English Grammar, Punctuation and Spelling Test code
2	Subordinating conjunctions	• Vocabulary, Grammar and Punctuation Skills Pupil Book 2, Grammar Unit 2, pages 18–19 • Vocabulary, Grammar and Punctuation Skills Teacher's Guide 2 – Grammar Unit 2, pages 39–41 – Photocopiable Grammar Unit 2, Resource 1: Finding subordinating conjunctions, page 87 – Photocopiable Grammar Unit 2, Resource 2: Subordinating conjunction sentences, page 88	Treasure House Vocabulary, Grammar and Punctuation Year 2, Grammar Unit 2	Subordination (using 'when', 'if', 'that', 'because') and coordination (using 'or', 'and', 'but')	G3.3 G3.4
3A	Expanded noun phrases to describe	• Vocabulary, Grammar and Punctuation Skills Pupil Book 2, Grammar Unit 3A, pages 20–21 • Vocabulary, Grammar and Punctuation Skills Teacher's Guide 2 – Grammar Unit 3A, pages 42–43 – Photocopiable Grammar Unit 3A, Resource 1: Finding nouns, page 89 – Photocopiable Grammar Unit 3A, Resource 2: Building expanded noun phrases, page 90	Treasure House Vocabulary, Grammar and Punctuation Year 2, Grammar Unit 3	Expanded noun phrases for description and specification [for example, 'the blue butterfly', 'plain flour', 'the man in the moon']	G3.2
3B	Expanding noun phrases to specify	• Vocabulary, Grammar and Punctuation Skills Pupil Book 2, Grammar Unit 3B, pages 22–23 • Vocabulary, Grammar and Punctuation Skills Teacher's Guide 2 – Grammar Unit 3B, pages 44–45 – Photocopiable Grammar Unit 3B, Resource 1: Ice-cream noun phrases, page 91 – Photocopiable Grammar Unit 3B, Resource 2: Noun phrases to specify, page 92	Treasure House Vocabulary, Grammar and Punctuation Year 2, Grammar Unit 3	Expanded noun phrases for description and specification [for example, 'the blue butterfly', 'plain flour', 'the man in the moon']	G3.2

Unit	Title	Treasure House Resources	Collins Connect	English Programme of Study	KS1 English Grammar, Punctuation and Spelling Test code

4	Sentence types: statements	• Vocabulary, Grammar and Punctuation Skills Pupil Book 2, Grammar Unit 4, pages 24–25
		• Vocabulary, Grammar and Punctuation Skills Teacher's Guide 2
		  – Grammar Unit 4, pages 46–47
		  – Photocopiable Grammar Unit 4, Resource 1: Is it a statement? page 93
		  – Photocopiable Grammar Unit 4, Resource 2: Writing statements, page 94
			Treasure House Vocabulary, Grammar and Punctuation Year 2, Grammar Unit 4	How the grammatical patterns in a sentence indicate its functions as a statement, question, exclamation or command	G2.1

5	Sentence types: questions	• Vocabulary, Grammar and Punctuation Skills Pupil Book 2, Grammar Unit 5, pages 26–27
		• Vocabulary, Grammar and Punctuation Skills Teacher's Guide 2
		  – Grammar Unit 5, pages 48–50
		  – Photocopiable Grammar Unit 5, Resource 1: Question words, page 95
		  – Photocopiable Grammar Unit 5, Resource 2: Questions, page 96
			Treasure House Vocabulary, Grammar and Punctuation Year 2, Grammar Unit 5	How the grammatical patterns in a sentence indicate its functions as a statement, question, exclamation or command	G2.2

6	Sentence types: exclamations	• Vocabulary, Grammar and Punctuation Skills Pupil Book 2, Grammar Unit 6, pages 28–29
		• Vocabulary, Grammar and Punctuation Skills Teacher's Guide 2
		  – Grammar Unit 6, pages 51–52
		  – Photocopiable Grammar Unit 6, Resource 1: Sorting exclamations, page 97
		  – Photocopiable Grammar Unit 6, Resource 2: Writing exclamations, page 98
			Treasure House Vocabulary, Grammar and Punctuation Year 2, Grammar Unit 6	How the grammatical patterns in a sentence indicate its functions as a statement, question, exclamation or command	G2.4

Unit	Title	Treasure House Resources	Collins Connect	English Programme of Study	KS1 English Grammar, Punctuation and Spelling Test code

7	Sentence types: commands	• Vocabulary, Grammar and Punctuation Skills Pupil Book 2, Grammar Unit 7, pages 30–31
		• Vocabulary, Grammar and Punctuation Skills Teacher's Guide 2
		  – Grammar Unit 7, pages 53–55
		  – Photocopiable Grammar Unit 7, Resource 1: Imperative verb search, page 99
		  – Photocopiable Grammar Unit 7, Resource 2: Commands, page 100
			Treasure House Vocabulary, Grammar and Punctuation Year 2, Grammar Unit 7	How the grammatical patterns in a sentence indicate its functions as a statement, question, exclamation or command	G2.3

8A	Past tense	• Vocabulary, Grammar and Punctuation Skills Pupil Book 2, Grammar Unit 8A, pages 32–33
		• Vocabulary, Grammar and Punctuation Skills Teacher's Guide 2
		  – Grammar Unit 8A, pages 56–57
		  – Photocopiable Grammar Unit 8A, Resource 1: Past or future tense, page 101
		  – Photocopiable Grammar Unit 8A, Resource 2: Yesterday, page 102
			Treasure House Vocabulary, Grammar and Punctuation Year 2, Grammar Unit 8	Correct choice and consistent use of present tense and past tense throughout writing	G4.2

8B	Present tense	• Vocabulary, Grammar and Punctuation Skills Pupil Book 2, Grammar Unit 8B, pages 34–35
		• Vocabulary, Grammar and Punctuation Skills Teacher's Guide 2
		  – Grammar Unit 8B, pages 58–59
		  – Photocopiable Grammar Unit 8B, Resource 1: Present tense verb search, page 103
		  – Photocopiable Grammar Unit 8B, Resource 2: Past and present tense sentences, page 104
			Treasure House Vocabulary, Grammar and Punctuation Year 2, Grammar Unit 8	Correct choice and consistent use of present tense and past tense throughout writing	G4.2

Unit	Title	Treasure House Resources	Collins Connect	English Programme of Study	KS1 English Grammar, Punctuation and Spelling Test code
9	Progressive verb forms in the present tense and past tense	• Vocabulary, Grammar and Punctuation Skills Pupil Book 2, Grammar Unit 9, pages 36–37 • Vocabulary, Grammar and Punctuation Skills Teacher's Guide 2 – Grammar Unit 9, pages 60–62 – Photocopiable Grammar Unit 9, Resource 1: Sorting tenses, page 105 – Photocopiable Grammar Unit 9, Resource 2: The volcano, page 106	Treasure House Vocabulary, Grammar and Punctuation Year 2, Grammar Unit 9	Use of the progressive form of verbs in the present and past tense to mark actions in progress [for example, 'she is drumming', 'he was shouting']	G1.2a
Punctuation					
A	Punctuation marks	• Vocabulary, Grammar and Punctuation Skills Pupil Book 2, Punctuation Unit A, pages 40–41 • Vocabulary, Grammar and Punctuation Skills Teacher's Guide 2 – Punctuation Unit A, pages 64–66 – Photocopiable Punctuation Unit A, Resource 1: Correcting sentences, page 107 – Photocopiable Punctuation Unit A, Resource 2: Writing sentences, page 108		Use of capital letters, full stops, question marks and exclamation marks to demarcate sentences	G6.1 G6.2 G6.3 G6.4
1	Commas in lists	• Vocabulary, Grammar and Punctuation Skills Pupil Book 2, Punctuation Unit 1, pages 42–43 • Vocabulary, Grammar and Punctuation Skills Teacher's Guide 2 – Punctuation Unit 1, pages 67–69 – Photocopiable Punctuation Unit 1, Resource 1: Adding commas to sentences, page 109 – Photocopiable Punctuation Unit 1, Resource 2: Making lists, page 110	Treasure House Vocabulary, Grammar and Punctuation Year 2, Punctuation Unit 1	Commas to separate items in a list	G6.5

Unit	Title	Treasure House Resources	Collins Connect	English Programme of Study	KS1 English Grammar, Punctuation and Spelling Test code

2	Apostrophes for omission	• Vocabulary, Grammar and Punctuation Skills Pupil Book 2, Punctuation Unit 2, pages 44–45
		• Vocabulary, Grammar and Punctuation Skills Teacher's Guide 2
		  – Punctuation Unit 2, pages 70–71
		  – Photocopiable Punctuation Unit 2, Resource 1: Matching contractions to whole words, page 111
		  – Photocopiable Punctuation Unit 2, Resource 2: Writing contractions, page 112
			Treasure House Vocabulary, Grammar and Punctuation Year 2, Punctuation Unit 2	Apostrophes to mark where letters are missing in spelling and to mark singular possession in nouns [for example, 'the girl's name']	G6.8

3	Apostrophes for possession	• Vocabulary, Grammar and Punctuation Skills Pupil Book 2, Punctuation Unit 3, pages 46–47
		• Vocabulary, Grammar and Punctuation Skills Teacher's Guide 2
		  – Punctuation Unit 3, pages 72–73
		  – Photocopiable Punctuation Unit 3, Resource 1: Showing possession, page 113
		  – Photocopiable Punctuation Unit 3, Resource 2: Using possessive apostrophes, page 114
			Treasure House Vocabulary, Grammar and Punctuation Year 2, Punctuation Unit 3	Apostrophes to mark where letters are missing in spelling and to mark singular possession in nouns [for example, 'the girl's name']	G6.8

Vocabulary Unit 1: Using suffixes to form nouns

Overview

English curriculum objectives

- Formation of nouns using suffixes such as –ness, –er and by compounding [for example, whiteboard, superman]

Treasure House resources

- Vocabulary, Grammar and Punctuation Skills Pupil Book 2, Vocabulary Unit 1, pages 4–5

- Collins Connect Treasure House Vocabulary, Grammar and Punctuation Year 2 Vocabulary, Unit 1
- Photocopiable Vocabulary Unit 1, Resource 1: –ness words word search, page 75
- Photocopiable Vocabulary Unit 1, Resource 2: –ness word sentences, page 76

Additional resources

- Poster paper, coloured pencils

Introduction

Teaching overview

This unit introduces children to the concept of forming nouns using suffixes, focusing specifically on adding the suffix '–ness' to adjectives and the suffix '–er' to verbs to form nouns. The suffix '–ness', added to adjectives, means the state of being the original adjective. For example, 'happiness' is 'the state of being happy'. The suffix '–er', when added to verbs to form nouns, indicates the doer of the root verb. For example, a 'crusher' is something that crushes, a 'teacher' is someone who teaches.

Use the content of this unit to actively develop children's oral vocabulary as well as their ability to understand and use the grammatical structures, giving particular support to children whose oral language skills are insufficiently developed. When modelling the teaching point, use your voice to show emphasis, intonation, tone, volume and natural speech patterns. This will help beginner learners to bridge the gaps between spoken and written vocabulary, grammar and punctuation.

Introduce the concept

Ask the children if any of them can tell you what a suffix is. Elicit ideas and establish that a suffix is a word ending that can be added to words to change their meaning. Write the suffix '–ness' on the board and tell the children that we can make nouns by adding this suffix to some words.

Write the word sums 'fit + –ness = fitness' and 'kind + –ness = kindness' on the board to demonstrate how '–ness' can be added to words to make nouns. Read the word sums with the children. Ask what type of word 'fit' (relating to health) is and elicit that it is an adjective. Ask what type of word 'fitness' is and elicit that it is a noun.

Discuss how the meaning of 'fit' is changed with the addition of the suffix '–ness' from a description to a thing: If you *are* fit, you *have* good fitness. Say some example sentences to demonstrate the change in meaning, for example, 'I used to be quite fit but my fitness got better when I started swimming.'

Repeat the process for the words 'kind' and 'kindness' and give some examples of the words in context, such as: 'The boy was kind and his kindness pleased his dad'. Explain to the children that, by completing the activities in the Pupil Book, they will learn about some more words that have the suffix '–ness' added to them.

Pupil practice

Pupil Book pages 4–5

Get started

The children copy sentences, then find and underline the words with the suffix '–ness'. You may wish to support the children by reading each sentence aloud, then pausing while they find and point to the words with the suffix '–ness', before asking them to copy the sentences.

Answers

1. *Amara's heart was filled with <u>sadness</u>.*   *[example]*

2. You can see the <u>goodness</u> in the old man's face.   [1 mark]

3. She used make-up to cover the <u>redness</u> of her sunburnt nose.   [1 mark]

4. The student's <u>rudeness</u> made the teacher angry.   [1 mark]

5. I wore sunglasses to protect my eyes from the <u>brightness</u> of the sun.   [1 mark]

Try these

The children copy and correct sentences by adding the suffix '–ness' to the words that do not make sense.

Answers

1. *I am suffering from an illness.*   *[example]*

2. Nervousness is natural before a test.   [1 mark]

3. Because of her shyness, she didn't want to be in the play.   [1 mark]

4. Some people suffer from seasickness.   [1 mark]

5. Is cleverness more important than honesty?   [1 mark]

Now try these

The children add the suffix '–ness' to the words 'careless' and 'polite' and then use them in sentences of their own. You may wish to support the children by discussing the task before setting them to work independently or in pairs.

Answers

1. Accept any sentence that includes the word 'carelessness' used in an appropriate context, for example, 'Her carelessness caused the accident.'
[2 marks: 1 mark for correctly adding the suffix; 1 mark for correct use of the word]

2. Accept any sentence that includes the word 'politeness' used in an appropriate context, for example, 'Politeness and good manners are important.'
[2 marks: 1 mark for correctly adding the suffix; 1 mark for correct use of the word]

Support, embed & challenge

Support

Use Vocabulary Unit 1 Resource 1: **–ness** words word search, to emphasise to the children the variety of words ending '–ness'. Ask the children to find the list of '–ness' words in the word search. Extend the task by asking the children to try to explain to a partner what each of the words in the word search mean. (**Answers** awareness, calmness, correctness, darkness, forgiveness, freshness, lateness, newness, rudeness, shyness, stubbornness and wetness)

f	o	r	g	i	v	e	n	e	s	s	d
r	a	u	n	e	u	l	e	v	t	j	k
e	h	d	q	f	r	y	w	c	u	v	b
s	m	e	r	b	j	s	n	g	b	o	d
h	l	n	k	x	m	d	e	o	b	w	a
n	w	e	t	n	e	s	s	t	o	x	r
e	g	s	h	y	n	e	s	s	r	i	k
s	p	s	e	t	q	n	h	c	n	w	n
s	l	a	t	e	n	e	s	s	n	z	e
s	u	i	a	w	a	r	e	n	e	s	s
c	o	r	r	e	c	t	n	e	s	s	s
c	a	l	m	n	e	s	s	a	s	f	p

Embed

Use Vocabulary Unit 1 Resource 2: **–ness** word sentences, to practise using words that end in the suffix '–ness' in sentences. Ask the children to fill the gaps in the sentences using words from the word box. Then ask them to use the '–ness' words to write their own sentences. Afterwards, ask volunteers to share the sentences they have written. (**Answers** 1. lateness, 2. smoothness, 3. weakness, 4. braveness, 5. cheerfulness)

Write the word sums 'teach + –er = teacher' and 'build + –er = builder' on the board to demonstrate how '–er' can be added to words to make nouns. Read the word sums with the children.

Ask what type of word 'teach' is and elicit that it is a verb. Ask: 'What am I doing right now?' Encourage the response that you are teaching. Ask: 'So what does that make me?' Encourage the response that you are a teacher. Ask what type of word 'teacher' is and elicit that it is a noun. Discuss how the meaning of 'teach' is changed with the addition of the suffix '–er' from an action to a thing that does the action: If you teach, you are a teacher.

Repeat the process for the words 'build' and 'builder'. Challenge the children to write sentences using 'teach' and 'teacher' and 'build' and 'builder', for example, 'You must be a patient teacher to teach grammar.', 'The builders will start to build our extension tomorrow.'

Challenge

Challenge these children to go on a hunt for the suffix '–ness'. Tell them to look through their reading book, or a selection of classroom books and note down examples of words they find that have the suffix '–ness'. Ask the children to make a poster to display the words they have found.

Homework / Additional activities

What happens next?

Ask the children to look at the word sums 'silly + –ness = silliness', 'happy + –ness = happiness', 'dirty + –ness = dirtiness' and work out what the rule is for adding the suffix '–ness' to words that end in the letter 'y'. (For root words of two syllables ending consonant + 'y', change the 'y' to an 'i'.)

Ask the children to list as many occupations that end '–er' as they can and to identify what each occupation involves (according to the root words), for example, a teacher teaches, a builder builds, a writer writes, a driver drives, a farmer farms.

Collins Connect: Vocabulary Unit 1

Ask the children to complete Vocabulary Unit 1 (see Teach → Year 2 → Vocabulary, Grammar and Punctuation → Vocabulary Unit 1).

Vocabulary Unit 2: Compound nouns

Overview

English curriculum objectives

- Formation of **nouns** using **suffixes** such as –ness, –er and by compounding [for example, whiteboard, superman]

Treasure House resources

- Vocabulary, Grammar and Punctuation Skills Pupil Book 2, Vocabulary Unit 2, pages 6–7
- Collins Connect Treasure House Vocabulary, Grammar and Punctuation Year 2, Vocabulary Unit 2

- Photocopiable Vocabulary Unit 2, Resource 1: Making compound nouns, page 77
- Photocopiable Vocabulary Unit 2, Resource 2: Compound noun definitions, page 78

Additional resources

- Compound noun props such as bags, brushes, boxes and balls (optional)

Introduction

Teaching overview

This unit introduces children to the concept of compound nouns. A compound noun is a noun that is made from two words put together. They are very common and new ones are being invented all the time. Most compound nouns comprise two nouns, such as 'bedroom', 'lightbulb' and 'football'. There are many other combinations but this unit focuses exclusively on compound nouns which consist of two nouns.

The meanings of compound nouns, while related to the meanings of their composite words, often differ crucially from or are more specific than the two original meanings. Usually, the first part of a compound noun describes its type or purpose and the second part identifies who or what. For example, a 'hairbrush' is for your hair and is a brush, a 'bedroom' is for your bed and is a room, a 'lightbulb' is a bulb of light. Compound nouns should be treated as one word.

Use the content of this unit to develop actively children's oral vocabulary as well as their ability to understand and use the grammatical structures, giving particular support to children whose oral language skills are insufficiently developed. When modelling the teaching point, use your voice to show emphasis, intonation, tone, volume and natural speech patterns. This will help beginner learners to bridge the gap between spoken and written vocabulary, grammar and punctuation.

Introduce the concept

The words 'tooth' and 'brush' are particularly good examples with which to introduce the concept of compound nouns because the meanings of the individual words 'tooth' and 'brush' can be expressed visually, using simple drawings. This should make it very clear to the children how the meanings of the words when separate are related to, but are different from, the meanings of the words when combined.

Write the words 'tooth' and 'brush' on the board. Draw a simple tooth shape under the word 'tooth' and draw a simple brush shape under the word 'brush'. Say: 'Here are two separate words, 'tooth' and 'brush'. But watch what happens when we put these two words together.' Write 'toothbrush' on the board and draw a simple toothbrush shape under the word. Show that you have made the new word 'toothbrush' by combining the two other words. Clarify the meanings of the three words 'tooth' (something with which we chew), 'brush' (something used for brushing) and 'toothbrush' (a brush for teeth). Say: 'This is called a "compound noun". A compound noun is a noun that is made from two words put together. Compound nouns can be treated as one word.'

Write the following word sums on the board: 'back + pack = backpack'; 'gold + fish = goldfish'. Then say example sentences to demonstrate the words being used in context: 'I carry my school bag on my back. It is a backpack.', 'The fish is a beautiful gold colour. It is a goldfish.'

Pupil practice

Pupil Book pages 6–7

Get started

The children copy sentences, then find and underline the compound nouns in each sentence. You may wish to support the children by reading each sentence aloud, then pausing while they find and point to the compound noun, before asking them to copy the sentences.

Answers

1. *I spread the <u>tablecloth</u> on the grass for a picnic.* *[example]*
2. I looked at my <u>eyebrows</u> in the mirror. [1 mark]
3. The <u>lighthouse</u> saved ships from crashing into the rocks. [1 mark]
4. I have a terrible <u>headache</u> today. [1 mark]
5. The <u>policewoman</u> caught the thief at the back of the shop. [1 mark]

Try these

The children copy and complete sentences using compound nouns made from a given selection of words.

Answers

1. *I love cleaning my teeth with this new toothpaste.* *[example]*
2. The postman delivered a parcel this morning. [1 mark]
3. My dad put on his sunglasses because it was sunny. [1 mark]
4. After eating lunch, we go outside and play in the school playground. [1 mark]
5. My mum had her keys in her handbag. [1 mark]

Now try these

The children write down which two words make up the compound nouns 'newspaper' and 'snowman'. They then use the words 'newspaper' and 'snowman' in sentences of their own. You may wish to support children by discussing the task before setting them to work independently or in pairs.

Answers

1. news, paper [1 mark] Accept any sentence that includes the word 'newspaper' used in an appropriate context, for example, 'Mum reads the newspaper every day.' [1 mark]
2. snow, man [1 mark] Accept any sentence that includes the word 'snowman' used in an appropriate context, for example, 'The children made a snowman in the garden.' [1 mark]

Support, embed & challenge

Support

Use Vocabulary Unit 2 Resource 1: Making compound nouns, to support these children in making compound nouns using a variety of separate words. Ask the children to match the words together to make as many compound nouns as they can and then to think of two more compound nouns. (**Answers** toybox, toothpaste, snowman, snowball, handbag, handball, postman, postbag, newsman, newspaper, rainbow, sunglasses)

Extend the activity by asking the children to discuss the meaning of each new word. You could ask them to write definitions or draw pictures to demonstrate the meanings.

Embed

Ask the children to take turns to think of a compound noun. (If they struggle, suggest one for them or ask them to make one from the words on Vocabulary Unit 2 Resource 1.) Each child provides clues to their compound noun either by drawing, miming or pointing to objects or body parts but without speaking. The other children must guess the word. Encourage them to provide two clues, one for each word their compound noun consists of. For example, they should show their teeth and then point to a brush for the word 'toothbrush', rather than simply mime brushing their teeth. You may wish to provide props such as bags, brushes, boxes and balls to inspire the children's choices and make giving clues a little easier.

Ask the children to work in pairs and provide each child with a copy of Vocabulary Unit 2 Resource 1: Making compound nouns. Ask them to cut the words out and spread them face down in front of them. They should then take turns to turn over two words. If the two words combined make a recognisable compound noun (in either order), they keep the words. Once all the words have been claimed (or there are no more combinations), the winner is the child with the most words.

Ask the children to carry out Vocabulary Unit 2 Resource 2: Compound noun definitions, matching compound nouns to their definitions.

(**Answers** 1. bedroom, 2. eyebrows, 3. shoelaces, 4. eggcup, 5. grandmother, 6. butterfly, 7. toenails, 8. sunshine, 9. raincoat, 10. teabag)

Challenge

Challenge the children to write a short, silly story using as many compound nouns as they can. You can either provide a list of compound nouns, ask them to use those on the resource sheets and in the Pupil Book, or challenge the children to remember and find their own selection.

Homework / Additional activities

What happens next?

Ask the children to go on a compound noun hunt to find as many compound nouns as they can. They could look in books, on the internet or ask friends and family. Make it a competition to find the most.

Collins Connect: Vocabulary Unit 2

Ask the children to complete Vocabulary Unit 2 (see Teach → Year 2 → Vocabulary, Grammar and Punctuation → Vocabulary Unit 2).

Vocabulary Unit 3: Using suffixes to form adjectives

Overview

English curriculum objectives
- Formation of adjectives using suffixes such as –ful, –less

Treasure House resources
- Vocabulary, Grammar and Punctuation Skills Pupil Book 2, Vocabulary Unit 3, pages 8–9

- Collins Connect Treasure House Vocabulary, Grammar and Punctuation Year 2, Vocabulary Unit 3
- Photocopiable Vocabulary Unit 3, Resource 1: –ful and –less words crossword, page 79
- Photocopiable Vocabulary Unit 3, Resource 2: –ful and –less word sentences, page 80

Introduction

Teaching overview

This unit introduces children to the concept of using suffixes to form adjectives. An adjective is a word that describes a noun or gives more information about it. We can make some useful adjectives by adding the suffixes '–ful' and '–less' to nouns: '–ful' means 'full of', for example, 'meaningful' means 'full of meaning' and 'painful' means 'full of pain'; the suffix '–less' means 'without', for example, 'meaningless' means 'without meaning' and 'painless' means 'without pain'.

Use the content of this unit to develop actively the children's oral vocabulary as well as their ability to understand and use the grammatical structures, giving particular support to children whose oral language skills are insufficiently developed. When modelling the teaching point, use your voice to show emphasis, intonation, tone, volume and natural speech patterns. This will help beginner learners to bridge the gap between spoken and written vocabulary, grammar and punctuation.

Introduce the concept

Ask the children if they can remember what we call word endings that are added to words to make them into new words. Establish that they are called suffixes and tell the children that in this lesson they will use the suffixes '–ful' and '–less' to make some new words. Explain that the words they make will be adjectives and that adjectives are very useful words. Adjectives help to describe nouns or give us more information.

Ask the children to imagine two brothers, one called Leo and the other called Luca. (You could even draw stick figure representations on the board, if you wish.) Ask the children to imagine Leo and Luca playing with their toys. Say: 'Do we know how Leo and Luca treat the toys?' Elicit that the answer is that we don't. Write the word 'care' on the board and say aloud (as if thinking to yourself): 'I wonder whether Leo and Luca care for their toys or not?' Then write 'care + –ful = careful' and write 'care + –less = careless'. Point to the words as you say: 'Leo was always careful with his toys. His brother Luca was careless and broke them!'

Re-emphasise the process of adding the suffixes '–ful' and '–less' to turn the word 'care' into 'careful' and 'careless'. Discuss what the addition of each suffix has done to the meaning of the word 'care': the addition of '–ful' changing 'care' from a verb to an adjective that means 'full of care' and '–less' changing 'care' from a verb to an adjective that means 'without care'.

Pupil practice

Pupil Book pages 8–9

Get started

The children copy sentences, then find and underline the adjectives with the suffixes '–ful' and '–less'. You may wish to support the children by reading each sentence aloud, then pausing while they find and point to the suffix '–ful' and '–less', before asking them to copy the sentences.

Answers

1. *My cat is <u>fearless</u> and he will climb any tree.* *[example]*
2. My dad loves <u>useful</u> gadgets. [1 mark]
3. The bird flew high up in the <u>cloudless</u> blue sky. [1 mark]
4. This situation is <u>hopeless</u>. There is nothing we can do. [1 mark]
5. The birds sang a <u>tuneful</u> song. [1 mark]

Try these

The children copy and correct sentences by adding the correct suffix, '–ful' or '–less', to the underlined words.

Answers

1. *The superhero was worried because his enemy was powerful.*   *[example]*
2. We thought the footballer was wonderful. [1 mark]
3. The kitchen floor was spotless after I cleaned it. [1 mark]
4. I was bored and restless because I had nothing to do. [1 mark]
5. When everyone is asleep in bed, the house is peaceful. [1 mark]

Now try these

The children add the suffixes '–ful' and '–less' to both the word 'pain' and the word 'colour'. They then write sentences of their own for all four new words. You may wish to support the children by discussing the task before setting them to work independently or in pairs.

Answers

1. Accept any two sentences that include the words 'painful' and 'painless' used in appropriate contexts, for example, 'Bee stings are painful.', 'The operation was painless.'

    [4 marks: 1 mark per correctly added suffix; 1 mark per correct use of the words]

2. Accept any two sentences that include the words 'colourful' and 'colourless' used in appropriate contexts, for example, 'Look at those colourful flowers!', 'He has a colourless personality.'

    [4 marks: 1 mark per correctly added suffix; 1 mark per correct use of the words]

Support, embed & challenge

Support

Use Vocabulary Unit 3 Resource 1: **–ful** and **–less** words crossword, to support these children in becoming more familiar with adjectives that end in the suffixes '–ful' and '–less'. Ask these children to solve the clues then write the words in the correct spaces on the crossword. (**Answers** across: 1. thankful, 2. tearful, 3. painful, 4. useful, 5. endless, 6. successful; down: 7. helpful, 8. fearless, 9. breathless, 10. playful)

Embed

Use Vocabulary Unit 3 Resource 2: **–ful** and **–less** word sentences, to develop the children's knowledge of adjectives that end in the suffixes '–ful' and '–less'. Ask the children to read the sentences and decide whether the missing word should be the one ending in '–ful' or '–less'. Then they should write the correct word in the gap. (**Answers** 1. useless, 2. thoughtful, 3. powerless, 4. hopeful, 5. tuneless, 6. colourful, 7. careless, 8. painless)

Challenge

Challenge these children to add the suffix '–ful' or '–less' to the words 'price', 'success', 'truth', 'thought', 'harm' and 'worth' and then use each word in sentences of their own devising. When they have finished, ask volunteers to share their sentences with the other children.

Homework / Additional activities

What happens next?

Ask the children to write a short, silly story about a school assembly. Ask them to try to include the words 'grateful', 'forceful', 'endless' and 'breathless'. Challenge them to include other '–ful' and '–less' words too.

Collins Connect: Vocabulary Unit 3

Ask the children to complete Vocabulary Unit 3 (see Teach → Year 2 → Vocabulary, Grammar and Punctuation → Vocabulary Unit 3).

Vocabulary Unit 4:
Using suffixes to form adverbs from adjectives

Overview

English curriculum objectives

- Use of the suffixes –er, –est in **adjectives** and the use of –ly in Standard English to turn adjectives into **adverbs**

Treasure House resources

- Vocabulary, Grammar and Punctuation Skills Pupil Book 2, Unit 4, pages 10–11

- Collins Connect Treasure House Vocabulary, Grammar and Punctuation Year 2, Vocabulary Unit 4
- Photocopiable Vocabulary Unit 4, Resource 1: Adverb word sums, page 81
- Photocopiable Vocabulary Unit 4, Resource 2: Sentence building, page 82

Additional resources

- Highlighters or coloured pencils

Introduction

Teaching overview

Adjectives are used to describe nouns. Adverbs are used to describe verbs. This unit introduces children to the concept of making adverbs from adjectives by adding the suffix '–ly', for example, 'sweet + –ly = sweetly', 'great + –ly = greatly'.

Use the content of this unit to develop actively children's oral vocabulary as well as their ability to understand and use the grammatical structures, giving particular support to children whose oral language skills are insufficiently developed. When modelling the teaching point, use your voice to show emphasis, intonation, tone, volume and natural speech patterns. This will help beginner learners to bridge the gap between spoken and written vocabulary, grammar and punctuation.

Introduce the concept

Write the word sum 'careful + –ly = carefully' on the board. Read the sum with the children, pointing to the words as you do so, and explain that the word 'carefully' is an adverb. Adverbs describe how things are done. We can make lots of adverbs from adjectives (such as 'careful') by adding the suffix '–ly'.

Say: 'Mr Ramdin carried the cup of tea carefully.' Clarify that the adverb 'carefully' describes how Mr Ramdin carried the cup of tea. Repeat the teaching point with a second example: Write the word sum 'loud + –ly = loudly' on the board and give the example sentence, 'She shouted loudly so they could hear her.'

Tell the children that in this lesson they will practise adding the suffix '–ly' to lots of adjectives to make adverbs.

Pupil practice

Get started

The children copy sentences, then find and underline the adverbs with the suffix '–ly'. You may wish to support the children by reading each sentence aloud, then pausing while they find and point to the suffix '–ly', before asking them to copy the sentences.

Answers

1. *She sang <u>softly</u> to the baby.*   *[example]*

2. He smiled <u>sweetly</u> at his friend.   [1 mark]

3. Izabel sniffed <u>sadly</u> as she sat alone.   [1 mark]

4. Calum stood up <u>bravely</u> in assembly.   [1 mark]

5. He spoke about his life <u>honestly</u>.   [1 mark]

Try these

The children make adverbs from adjectives by adding the suffix '–ly'. They then use each new word in sentences of their own.

Answers

1. *She stared <u>rudely</u> at the man.*   *[example]*

2. Accept any sentence that includes the word 'secretly' used in an appropriate context, for example, 'The meeting was secretly recorded.'
[2 marks: 1 mark for correctly adding the suffix; 1 mark for correct use of the word]

3. Accept any sentence that includes the word 'quietly' used in an appropriate context, for example, 'They came into the house quietly.'
[2 marks: 1 mark for correctly adding the suffix; 1 mark for correct use of the word]

4. Accept any sentence that includes the word 'sadly' used in an appropriate context, for example, 'The children walked home sadly after coming last in the dance competition.'
[2 marks: 1 mark for correctly adding the suffix; 1 mark for correct use of the word]

5. Accept any sentence that includes the word 'badly' used in an appropriate context, for example, 'They played badly in the final match.'
[2 marks: 1 mark for correctly adding the suffix; 1 mark for correct use of the word]

Now try these

The children rewrite sentences by adding adverbs with '–ly' to improve them. You may wish to support children by discussing the task before setting them to work independently or in pairs.

Answers

1. Accept any appropriate adverb added, for example, 'The lady spoke politely to the children.'   [1 mark]

2. Accept any appropriate adverb added, for example, 'The children watched the film quietly.'   [1 mark]

3. Accept any appropriate adverb added, for example, 'The man crossed the road carefully.'   [1 mark]

Support, embed & challenge

Support

Use Vocabulary Unit 4 Resource 1: Adverb word sums, to support these children in practising reading, writing and understanding words that end in '–ly' where no change has been made to the root word. (**Answers** 1. *slowly*, 2. quickly, 3. dangerously, 4. truthfully, 5. gladly, 6. madly, 7. delicately, 8. sternly, 9. firmly, 10. honestly)

Afterwards, use the resource sheet to discuss the spellings, pronunciation and meanings of the words. Extend the task by working with these children to put some of the words into sentences, either orally or written.

Embed

Write the sentence 'The wise queen rules wisely.' for the children to see. Ask: 'Which word is the noun?' Elicit that 'queen' is the noun in this sentence. Ask: 'What adjective describes the queen?' Elicit that 'wise' is the adjective that describes the queen. Ask: 'What does the queen do?' Elicit that the queen 'rules' and encourage the children to spot that this is a verb. Ask: 'How does she rule?' Elicit that she rules 'wisely' and encourage the children to spot that this is an adverb.

Repeat the process with the sentences: 'The bright stars twinkle brightly.', 'The quiet mice scamper quietly.', 'The noisy children play noisily.' Add any more sentences you think are useful.

Help the children to understand that adjectives describe things and adverbs describe actions so, to describe how something is done, they can add '–ly' to an adjective.

Ask the children to copy the sentences and underline or highlight the nouns in dark green, the adjectives in light green, the verbs in dark blue and the adverbs in light blue.

Use Vocabulary Unit 4 Resource 2: Sentence building, to help the children to think more about how to use adverbs ending in '–ly'. Ask the children to select actions from Box A, select adverbs from Box B and then use them together to build sentences of their own.

Challenge

Challenge these children to find as many '–ly' adverbs as they can. Then ask them to make a poster to display them. Tell these children to try to explain the spelling rule for adding '–ly' to words that end in '–le', using the words on their posters as examples. (The rule is to remove '–le' and add '–ly'.) If you haven't taught this rule for spelling yet, you could explain it once the children have attempted to work it out or, if they struggle, you could provide them with some word sums, such as 'sparkle + –ly = sparkly', 'gentle + –ly = gently'.

Homework / Additional activities

What happens next?

Ask the children to talk to their parents about the suffix '–ly' and to find examples of it in their reading books. Ask them to find as many words ending '–ly' as they can. They could look in books, on the internet or ask friends and family. Make it a competition to find the most. Ask them to bring a list of the words they find to school to share with the class.

Collins Connect: Vocabulary Unit 4

Ask the children to complete Vocabulary Unit 4 (see Teach → Year 2 → Vocabulary, Grammar and Punctuation → Vocabulary Unit 4).

Vocabulary Unit 5: Using suffixes in adjectives

Overview

English curriculum objectives

- Use of the suffixes –er, –est in **adjectives** and the use of –ly in Standard English to turn adjectives into **adverbs**

Treasure House resources

- Vocabulary, Grammar and Punctuation Skills Pupil Book 2, Vocabulary Unit 5, pages 12–13

- Collins Connect Treasure House Vocabulary, Grammar and Punctuation Year 2, Vocabulary Unit 5
- Photocopiable Vocabulary Unit 5, Resource 1: Comparative sentences, page 83
- Photocopiable Vocabulary Unit 5, Resource 2: Comparisons quiz, page 84

Additional resources

- Poster paper, coloured pencils

Introduction

Teaching overview

This unit introduces children to the concept of creating comparative adjectives by adding the suffixes '–er' (for example, 'warm + –er = warmer') and '–est' (for example, 'warm + –est = warmest'). The suffix '–er' is used when comparing two things, for example, 'Today is hotter than yesterday.' The suffix '–est' is used when describing a thing that is the most or least of something in a group and should be used with 'the', for example, 'Today is the hottest day of the year, so far.' The words 'more' and 'most' are never used with adjectives ending '–er' or '–est', for example, 'more faster' or 'most fastest' are incorrect. The '–er' or '–est' ending isn't normally added to adjectives of two syllables ending '–ful' or to adjectives of three or more syllables so these adjectives are used with the words 'more' and 'most' when used to make comparisons, for example, 'more dangerous', 'the most hateful'.

Use the content of this unit to actively develop children's oral vocabulary as well as their ability to understand and use the grammatical structures, giving particular support to children whose oral language skills are insufficiently developed. When modelling the teaching point, use your voice to show emphasis, intonation, tone, volume and natural speech patterns. This will help beginner learners to bridge the gaps between spoken and written vocabulary, grammar and punctuation.

Introduce the concept

Explain to the children that adjectives can be used to compare people or things by adding the suffixes '–er' and '–est'. Write 'small' on the board. Ask: 'What sort of word is this?' Elicit that it is an adjective. Explain to the children that, to use this adjective to compare two things, '–er' must be added to the end. Write the word sum 'small + er = smaller'. Say an example sentence or two (such as, 'Mice are smaller than elephants') and ask volunteers to think of examples too. Repeat the process with more adjectives such as 'smart', 'cold' and 'tall'.

Tell the children that, to use an adjective to describe something as the most or least of something, '–est' must be added to the end. Write the word 'fast'. Ask: 'How would I say that a girl runs faster than everyone else in her class?' Elicit that you would use the word 'fastest' and say the example sentence 'Chloe is the fastest runner in her class.' Tell the children that 'the' is used with adjectives that end '–est'. Repeat the process with more adjectives, such as 'soft', 'hard' and 'young'. Invite volunteers to contribute example sentences, ensuring they use 'the' before the superlative adjective.

Draw a table with three columns on the board. Give columns two and three the headings '–er' and '–est' and write the adjectives you have looked at so far in the left columns. Invite volunteers to fill in the comparative and superlative adjectives. Use the table to construct sentences that use all three adjectives, such as: 'Those books are cheap, that book is cheaper and this book is the cheapest.', 'Javier is tall, Fortis is taller but Amelia is the tallest.' (You could ask the children from your class to stand up and model 'tall', 'taller' and 'tallest'.) Tell the children that, in this lesson, they will practise using words that end in the suffixes '–er' and '–est' to compare people and things.

Pupil practice

Pupil Book pages 12–13

Get started

The children copy sentences, then find and underline the comparing adjectives. You may wish to support the children by reading each sentence aloud, then pausing while they find and point to the comparing adjectives, before asking them to copy the sentences.

Answers

1. *In England, July is* <u>warmer</u> *than January.* [example]

2. Sally is the <u>tallest</u> student in our class. [1 mark]

3. Your hands feel <u>colder</u> than my hands. [1 mark]

4. Our house is the <u>smallest</u> on the street. [1 mark]

5. That car is <u>cheaper</u> than this car. [1 mark]

Try these

The children copy and complete sentences using one of two given comparisons for each sentence. Before they begin, explain to the children that the word 'more' is never used with an adjective that has an '–er' or '–est' ending. Also explain that the '–er' or '–est' ending isn't normally added to adjectives of two syllables ending '–ful' or to adjectives of three or more syllables so these adjectives are used with the word 'more' when used to make comparisons. Remind children of the spelling rule: 'y' is changed to 'i' before '–er' and '–est'.

Answers

1. *Sienna tried harder than Jo did.* [example]

2. The butterfly is even more beautiful than the flower! [1 mark]

3. Are alligators more dangerous than crocodiles? [1 mark]

4. Mrs Sanchez's voice is louder than Mr Rodrigues' voice. [1 mark]

5. The kitten is naughtier than the cat. [1 mark]

Now try these

The children add the suffixes '–er' and '–est' to both the word 'big' and the word 'angry'. They then write comparing sentences of their own to use all four new words. You may wish to support children by discussing the task before setting them to work independently or in pairs.

Answers

1. Accept any two sentences that include the words 'bigger' and 'biggest' used in appropriate contexts, for example, 'The new car is bigger than the old car.', 'The African elephant is the biggest land animal.'

[4 marks: 1 mark per correctly added suffix; 1 mark per correct use of the words]

2. Accept any two sentences that include the words 'angrier' and 'angriest' used in appropriate contexts, for example, 'Mum was angrier than Dad when I told them the truth.', 'We were all angry but Ail was the angriest.'

[4 marks: 1 mark per correctly added suffix; 1 mark per correct use of the words]

Support, embed & challenge

Support

Use Vocabulary Unit 5 Resource 1: Comparative sentences, to support these children in using adjectives ending in the suffixes '–er' and '–est' when comparing people and things. Model reading the example sentence. Point out that the other sentences follow the same pattern. Read the other sentences aloud, emphasising the pattern they all follow and pausing before the gaps to encourage the children to join in with you and say what should fill the gaps. Support children to spell the missing words in the sentences as necessary. (**Answers** 1. *taller, the tallest*, 2. faster, the fastest, 3. brighter, the brightest, 4. colder, the coldest, 5. older, the oldest, 6. smaller, the smallest, 7. softer, the softest, 8. louder, the loudest)

Embed

Use Vocabulary Unit 5 Resource 2: Comparisons quiz, to encourage the children to use words ending in the suffix '–est' when comparing the children in the class. Ask the children to find out (by asking one another or by making a judgement) who is the tallest, youngest, oldest, loudest, fastest, smallest, kindest and calmest in their class and record the names of the children on the sheet. Then children should write three of their own sentences to compare attributes of their own choosing.

Challenge

Challenge these children to make a bold, colourful poster for the classroom that teaches other children about using the suffixes '–er' and '–est' to compare things.

Homework / Additional activities

What happens next?

Ask the children to look around their homes for things to compare and to write ten sentences comparing things.

Collins Connect: Vocabulary Unit 5

Ask the children to complete Vocabulary Unit 5 (see Teach → Year 2 → Vocabulary, Grammar and Punctuation → Vocabulary Unit 5).

Review unit 1: Vocabulary

A. Children copy and correct the sentences. They add the suffix '–ness' to the word that doesn't make sense.

1. My fitness has improved since I have been running every day. [1 mark]
2. With the light off, the room was plunged into darkness. [1 mark]
3. Everyone says there is a strong likeness between Dot and her mum. [1 mark]
4. I suffer from travel sickness on long car journeys. [1 mark]
5. Gran has a weakness for chocolate. [1 mark]

B. Children match the words together to make compound nouns.

   rainbow, haircut, hairball, flyball, football, butterball, butterfly, ballroom, bedroom [1 mark]

C. Children copy and correct the sentences by adding the correct suffix, '–ful' or '–less', to the underlined words.

1. After the race, Sally felt <u>breathless</u>. [1 mark]
2. Dominic's new puppy was really <u>playful</u>. [1 mark]
3. Mrs Jameson was <u>grateful</u> to the children for tidying her garden. [1 mark]
4. There was nothing the sailor could do, he was completely <u>helpless</u>. [1 mark]
5. Joshua couldn't wait to get home as his new school shoes were really <u>painful</u>. [1 mark]

D. Children make adverbs from the adjectives by adding the suffix '–ly'. They then write sentences of their own with the new words.

1. wisely [1 mark]
2. safely [1 mark]
3. slowly [1 mark]
4. quickly [1 mark]
5. cheaply [1 mark]

E. Children copy and complete the sentences by choosing the correct comparison from the box.

1. Mr Moneybags was the richest man in the town. [1 mark]
2. The clown was funnier than the comedian. [1 mark]
3. As the sun rose, the sky became lighter. [1 mark]
4. My little brother is the noisiest child you will ever meet! [1 mark]
5. This March has been the wettest month in years. [1 mark]

Grammar Unit 1: Coordinating conjunctions

Introduction

Teaching overview

Conjunctions are joining words. They link parts of sentences. This unit introduces children to the concept of joining two independent sentences by using the coordinating conjunctions 'and', 'or' and 'but'. The words 'and', 'but' and 'or' are the three main coordinating conjunctions. They are used to join what would be two grammatically independent clauses (phrases that could make complete sentences) as a single sentence. For example, the two sentences 'I enjoy surfing.' and 'I am afraid of sharks.' can be joined using 'but': 'I enjoy surfing but I am afraid of sharks.'

The addition of a conjunction adds meaning by indicating how the two independent clauses are linked: 'and' is used to list things or ideas; 'or' is used to discuss alternatives; 'but' is used to contrast facts or ideas. With the addition of a coordinating conjunction, some details can be omitted from the second clause, for example, 'I enjoy surfing but am afraid of sharks.'

Use the content of this unit to actively develop children's oral vocabulary as well as their ability to understand and use the grammatical structures, giving particular support to children whose oral language skills are insufficiently developed. When modelling the teaching point, use your voice to show emphasis, intonation, tone, volume and natural speech patterns. This will help beginner learners to bridge the gaps between spoken and written vocabulary, grammar and punctuation.

Introduce the concept

Ask the children: 'If we want to join two sentences together, what joining words could we use to do that?' Elicit ideas. Discuss why sentences might need joining together. Elicit that it could be to avoid too many short sentences or that it might be to show a relationship between the sentences.

Write the following sentences on the board with a line drawn in the middle as shown: 'I like fruit. _____ I like sweets.', 'I can play football. _____ I can go swimming.', 'I have my coat. _____ I forgot my hat.'

Tell the children that we can use coordinating conjunctions to join two sentences together. The main coordinating conjunctions are 'and', 'or' and 'but'. Write the words 'and', 'or' and 'but' on the board. Ask the children to help you work out which coordinating conjunction works best in each sentence. Rub out the full stops after the first sentences. Read the sentences aloud and insert each word in the gaps to see which sounds best.

Tell the children that we use 'and' to make a list ('I like fruit and I like sweets.'), 'or' to show alternatives ('I can play football or I can go swimming.') and 'but' to contrast ('I have my coat but I forgot my hat.').

Pupil practice

Pupil Book pages 16–17

Get started

The children copy sentences, then find and underline the coordinating conjunctions. You may wish to support the children by reading each sentence aloud, then pausing while they find and point to the coordinating conjunctions, before asking them to copy the sentences.

Answers

1. We could watch tennis <u>or</u> we could watch cartoons. *[example]*

2. I am tired <u>but</u> I don't want to go bed. [1 mark]

3. They put their pens away <u>and</u> they closed their books. [1 mark]

4. They could have cheese <u>or</u> they could have tuna. [1 mark]

5. I had a new toy <u>but</u> my sister broke it. [1 mark]

Try these

The children put words in the correct order to make sentences. If they struggle, remind them that sentences start with a capital letter, end with a full stop and that coordinating conjunctions usually appear somewhere in the middle. Encourage them to start with what they are sure of and then fill in the rest of the words.

Answers

1. *We could play inside or we could play outside.* [example]

2. I would like to play outside but it is raining.[1 mark]

3. We could choose oranges or we could choose apples. / We could choose apples or we could choose oranges. [1 mark]

4. I'll have a party but I won't have a sleepover. / I'll have a sleepover but I won't have a party. [1 mark]

5. My dad is sleeping and he is snoring. [1 mark]

Now try these

The children join pairs of sentences with the most appropriate coordinating conjunction: 'and', 'or' or 'but'. You may wish to support children by discussing the task before setting them to work independently or in pairs.

1. I like carrots but I do not like peppers. [1 mark]

2. I could play on the swings first or I could play on the slide first. [1 mark]

Support, embed & challenge

Support

Use Grammar Unit 1 Resource 1: Building coordinating conjunction sentences, to support these children in learning to use coordinating conjunctions to make longer sentences. Ask the children to cut out all the sentence parts and coordinating conjunctions then match them together to build longer sentences and stick them down to another piece of paper. Encourage the children to discuss which of the coordinating conjunctions works best within each sentence. (**Answers** I like toast for breakfast but I like eggs more than toast. We could go to the park or we could go to the shops. I got a new coat and I got new boots. You can choose an ice lolly or you can choose ice cream. They said it would rain but it has been sunny all day. I finished my homework and I tidied my room. Accept other combinations if they make sense.)

Embed

Ask the children to work in pairs. Provide texts or ask the children to look through their reading books for examples of sentences with coordinating conjunctions. Ask the pairs to share and discuss what they find.

Draw a table on the board for the children to copy and complete with the headings "and' for a list', "or' for a choice', "but' to compare'. Ask the children to fill in the table with the examples they have found and underline the coordinating conjunction in each sentence.

Use Grammar Unit 1 Resource 2: Finishing coordinating conjunction sentences, to provide practice using coordinating conjunctions by completing sentences. Ask the children to read the first part of each sentence, decide which coordinating conjunction they will use ('and', 'but' or 'or') and then finish the sentence in their own words. Tell them that they may need to go back and change the conjunction after they have written the sentence if they realise a different one would have worked better.

Challenge

Challenge these children to write three sentences about an imaginary shopping trip. Tell them to use a different coordinating conjunction, 'and', 'but', or 'or', in each sentence.

Homework / Additional activities

What happens next?

Ask the children to talk with their family and friends about coordinating conjunctions. Challenge them to find one example of each, 'and', 'but' and 'or', and write the sentences down to share with the class.

Collins Connect: Grammar Unit 1

Ask the children to complete Grammar Unit 1 (see Teach → Year 2 → Vocabulary, Grammar and Punctuation → Grammar Unit 1).

Grammar Unit 2: Subordinating conjunctions

Overview

English curriculum objectives
- Subordination (using 'when', 'if', 'that', 'because') and coordination (using 'or', 'and', 'but')

Treasure House resources
- Vocabulary, Grammar and Punctuation Skills Pupil Book 2, Grammar Unit 2, pages 18–19
- Collins Connect Treasure House Vocabulary, Grammar and Punctuation Year 2, Grammar Unit 2

- Photocopiable Grammar Unit 2, Resource 1: Finding subordinating conjunctions, page 87
- Photocopiable Grammar Unit 2, Resource 2: Subordinating conjunction sentences, page 88

Additional resources
- Different coloured pens (for Resource sheet 1)
- Texts in which to find examples of sentences with subordinating conjunctions

Introduction

Teaching overview

Conjunctions are joining words. They link parts of sentences. This unit introduces children to the concept of using the subordinating conjunctions 'because', 'if', 'when' and 'that' to join clauses when the second clause relies on the first clause for its meaning.

The addition of a conjunction adds meaning by indicating how the clauses are linked: 'because' indicates that the subordinate clause is a reason for the main clause (for example, 'I'm not going surfing because there are sharks in the water.'); 'if' indicates that the subordinate clause is a condition of the main clause (for example, 'I'm not going surfing if there are sharks in the water.'); 'when' indicates that the subordinate clause is a circumstance in which the first clause happens (for example, 'I'm not going surfing when there are sharks in the water.'); 'that' introduces a thought or statement pertaining to the first clause ('I told you that there are sharks in the water.') (In informal English, 'that' is often left out.) Subordinating clauses can usually go first or last in a sentence, for example, 'Because there are sharks in the water, I'm not going surfing.' However, in this unit, they are placed last.

Use the content of this unit to actively develop children's oral vocabulary as well as their ability to understand and use the grammatical structures, giving particular support to children whose oral language skills are insufficiently developed. When modelling the teaching point, use your voice to show emphasis, intonation, tone, volume and natural speech patterns. This will help beginner learners to bridge the gap between spoken and written vocabulary, grammar and punctuation.

Introduce the concept

Ask the children to remind you of the coordinating conjunctions or joining words that they already know. Elicit 'and', 'but' and 'or'. Remind them that the two sentences that were joined together using those words made sense on their own – they were equal. Explain that today they will learn how to join sentences together when the second sentence relies on, or needs, the first sentence to help it make sense. Tell them that the words they will use to join the sentences together are called 'subordinating' conjunctions.

On the board, write 'because', 'if', 'when' and 'that' and tell the children that these are the subordinating conjunctions they will be using. Write the following sentences on the board: 'I love my birthday because people give me presents.', 'You can get cold if you forget to wear a coat.', 'I never cry when I fall off my bike.', 'I promised my mum that I would play carefully.'

Read the sentences with the children but say the second part of each sentence to the children first to show that it needs the first part to help it make sense. You may like to ask the children to repeat the sentences after you to help them practise using vocabulary and sentence structures that they may not already have within their daily vocabulary.

Pupil practice

Pupil Book pages 18–19

Get started

The children copy sentences, then find and underline the subordinating conjunction in each. You may wish to support the children by reading each sentence aloud, then pausing while they find and point to the subordinating conjunction, before asking them to copy the sentences.

Answers

1. *I am at Grandma's house <u>because</u> Mum is working.* [example]

2. I am happy <u>that</u> the sun is shining. [1 mark]

3. They went to bed <u>when</u> it got dark. [1 mark]

4. I have an apple for breakfast <u>because</u> I love fruit. [1 mark]

5. I will play with her <u>if</u> she is kind. [1 mark]

Try these

The children copy and complete sentences using 'because', 'if', 'when' or 'that'.

Answers

1. *I said that Jamal could borrow my red pen.* [example]

2. It is warmest in England when it is summer. [1 mark]

3. I can have a party next week if I am good. [1 mark]

4. My dad is napping because he is tired. [1 mark]

5. Our teacher told us that we had passed our test. [1 mark]

Now try these

The children finish sentences by adding extra information after the subordinating conjunction. You may wish to support children by discussing the task before setting them to work independently or in pairs.

Answers

1. Accept any appropriate main clauses, for example, 'You will get hot if you sit in the sun.' Ensure that it is not treated as a relative pronoun in this context. [1 mark]

2. Accept any appropriate main clauses, for example, 'I was late because I missed the bus.' Ensure that it is not treated as a relative pronoun in this context. [1 mark]

3. Accept any appropriate main clauses, for example, 'We could go out to play when it stops raining.' Ensure that it is not treated as a relative pronoun in this context. [1 mark]

4. Accept any appropriate main clauses, 'for example, 'Sidney told his dad that he was sorry for breaking the window.' Ensure that it is not treated as a relative pronoun in this context. [1 mark]

Support, embed & challenge

Support

Use Grammar Unit 2 Resource 1: Finding subordinating conjunctions, to support these children in practising reading, identifying and understanding the subordinating conjunctions 'because', 'if', 'that' and 'when'. Ask the children to find and draw a circle around the subordinating conjunctions 'because', 'if', 'when' and 'that', then underline the first and second parts of each sentence using different colours. (**Answers** 1. <u>I love my birthday</u> **because** <u>I have a party.</u> 2. <u>You might get hot</u> **if** <u>you keep your jumper on all day.</u> 3. <u>I always cry</u> **when** <u>I watch a sad film.</u> 4. <u>I told my dad</u> **that** <u>I would be home by six o'clock.</u> 5. <u>I am at after-school club</u> **because** <u>Dad is running late.</u> 6. <u>I am excited</u> **that** <u>it is snowing.</u> 7. <u>We woke up</u> **when** <u>the birds started singing.</u> 8. <u>I eat toast for breakfast</u> **because** <u>I'm not keen on cereal.</u>)

Embed

Ask the children to work in pairs. Provide texts or ask the children to look through their reading books for examples of sentences with subordinating conjunctions. Ask the pairs to share and discuss what they find. Draw a table on the board for the children to copy and complete with the headings "because' for a reason', "if' for a condition', "when' for a circumstance'. Ask the children to fill in the table with the examples they have found and underline the subordinating conjunction in each sentence.

Use Grammar Unit 2 Resource 2: Subordinating conjunction sentences, to encourage the children to practise reading, understanding and applying the subordinating conjunctions. Ask the children to read the sentences and fill the gaps with the most suitable subordinating conjunctions.

(Answers 1. It is coldest in England when it is winter. 2. I said that Jamal could come to my house for tea. 3. I can play at Jessie's house next week if I get all my homework finished first. 4. My grandad is gardening because he enjoys it. 5. Our teacher told us that we are going to visit the museum. 6. We could practise our play when we have finished our writing. 7. I was reading a book because I had some spare time. 8. India told us that she is going on holiday. Accept other choices if they make sense.)

Challenge

Challenge these children to write four sentences about an imaginary visit to a museum. Ask them to use a different subordinating conjunction ('that', 'if', 'when' or 'because') in each sentence.

Homework / Additional activities

What happens next?

Ask the children to talk to their parents about the subordinating conjunctions 'that', 'if', 'when' and 'because'. Ask parents to help their child spot these words in books they read at home or signs they see when outside.

Collins Connect: Grammar Unit 2

Ask the children to complete Grammar Unit 2 (see Teach → Year 2 → Vocabulary, Grammar and Punctuation → Grammar Unit 2).

Grammar Unit 3A: Expanded noun phrases to describe

Overview

English curriculum objectives

- Expanded noun phrases for description and specification [for example, 'the blue butterfly', 'plain flour', 'the man in the moon']

Treasure House resources

- Vocabulary, Grammar and Punctuation Skills Pupil Book 2, Grammar Unit 3A, pages 20–21

- Collins Connect Treasure House Vocabulary, Grammar and Punctuation Year 2, Grammar Unit 3
- Photocopiable Grammar Unit 3A, Resource 1: Finding nouns, page 89
- Photocopiable Grammar Unit 3A, Resource 2: Building expanded noun phrases, page 90

Additional resources

- Objects and pictures to describe

Introduction

Teaching overview

This unit introduces children to the concept of expanding noun phrases to describe people and things. A noun phrase is a group of words that work together and contain a noun, for example, 'an apple'. Noun phrases can be expanded with the addition of adjectives and additional information to describe the noun, for example, 'the red apple'.

Use the content of this unit to actively develop children's oral vocabulary as well as their ability to understand and use the grammatical structures, giving particular support to children whose oral language skills are insufficiently developed. When modelling the teaching point, use your voice to show emphasis, intonation, tone, volume and natural speech patterns. This will help beginner learners to bridge the gap between spoken and written vocabulary, grammar and punctuation.

Introduce the concept

On the board, write the word 'rabbit'. Read it aloud slowly and clearly and ask the children: 'What type of word is this?' Pause to allow the children to think and then take suggestions. Establish that it is a noun (a common noun).

Explain to the children that, if they were writing about a rabbit, just calling it a 'rabbit' doesn't give the reader much information. Show how you can expand the noun by adding other words and phrases, for example, 'rabbit' → 'the rabbit' → 'the happy rabbit' → 'the happy rabbit in the field'.

Tell the children that we can put adjectives in front of nouns to describe them and we can also add descriptive details after nouns. Ask the children to help you think of words and phrases that could be used to describe a cat, a mouse, a house, a castle, a tree, a forest and so on.

Pupil practice

Pupil Book pages 20–21

Get started

The children copy phrases, then find and underline the noun being described. You may wish to support the children by reading each sentence aloud, then pausing while they find and point to the noun that is being described, before asking them to copy the phrases.

Answers

1. the glass <u>vase</u>   *[example]*
2. the purple <u>jumper</u>   [1 mark]
3. the useful little <u>gadget</u>   [1 mark]
4. the <u>house</u> with the creaking door [1 mark]
5. that cheerful little <u>girl</u> in the nursery [1 mark]

Try these

The children copy and complete sentences by choosing the best words from the boxes to fill the gaps.

Answers

1. *I would like a refreshing drink.*   *[example]*
2. We have bought a new game.   [1 mark]
3. We played in the muddy field.   [1 mark]
4. My dad is riding the bike with the red basket. [1 mark]
5. My friend Lucy is the dancer with the curly hair. [1 mark]

Now try these

The children describe the nouns 'car' and 'chair' using adjectives to give extra information. They then use the noun phrases they have created in sentences. You may wish to support children by discussing their sentences before setting them to work independently.

Answers

Accept any sentences that expand the given nouns with appropriate adjectives and/or descriptive prepositional or adverbial phrases. Award marks for each descriptive detail and for the sentences.

[4 marks]

1. Accept any sentence that expands the noun 'car' with appropriate adjectives and/or descriptive prepositional or adverbial phrases, for example, 'Dad's got a new car with black leather seats.'
   [2 marks: 1 mark for an expanded noun phrase; 1 mark for a sentence that correctly uses the expanded noun phrase]

2. Accept any sentence that expands the noun 'chair' with appropriate adjectives and/or descriptive prepositional or adverbial phrases, for example, 'There's an old wooden chair with no arms in the kitchen.'
   [2 marks: 1 mark for an expanded noun phrase; 1 mark for a sentence that correctly uses the expanded noun phrase]

Support, embed & challenge

Support

Use Grammar Unit 3A Resource 1: Finding nouns, to support these children in practising identifying the noun that is being described. Ask the children to read the sentences on the sheet and circle the noun that is being described. (**Answers** 1. dragon, 2. teapot, 3. supermarket, 4. curry, 5. envelope, 6. pen, 7. baby, 8. juice)

The sentences also provide models for the children to see how noun phrases can be expanded. Spend some time discussing these, looking at the adjectives before the nouns and the additional information given after the nouns.

There is an additional activity at the bottom of the worksheet that gives the children the opportunity to write their own expanded noun phrases using the nouns 'T-shirt', 'book' and 'car'.

Embed

Use Grammar Unit 3A Resource 2: Building expanded noun phrases, to enable children to explore building their own expanded noun phrases to describe nouns. Ask the children to make expanded noun phrases by choosing a noun from the first box then choosing words and phrases to describe their

noun from the second box. They can also add their own descriptions, should they wish to. Tell them to write their phrases on the lines underneath.

Organise the children into groups and give each group a selection of pictures and objects. Ask them to look at the pictures and objects and, working together as a group, write phrases to describe what they see, for example, 'a yellow beach ball', 'a blue mug with a missing handle'. Once the groups have written descriptions of all their objects and pictures, ask each group to share their descriptions. Discuss their vocabulary choices and invite volunteers to suggest any additional details they could have included.

Challenge

Ask the children to write three sentences about items that could be found in a school. Suggest they describe the items in as much detail as possible using adjectives before the nouns and providing extra information after them. Encourage them not to repeat themselves either by using adjectives with the same meanings, such as 'loud, noisy children', or by adding information that is already in the noun, such as 'the enormous giant'.

Homework / Additional activities

What happens next?

Ask the children to search for expanded noun phrases that describe. They could look in books, on the internet or ask friends and family. Make it a competition to find the most.

Collins Connect: Grammar Unit 3

Ask the children to complete Grammar Unit 3 (see Teach → Year 2 → Vocabulary, Grammar and Punctuation → Grammar Unit 3).

Note: the Collins Connect activities could be used with Unit 3A or 3B.

Grammar Unit 3B: Expanded noun phrases to specify

Overview

English curriculum objectives
- Expanded noun phrases for description and specification [for example, 'the blue butterfly', 'plain flour', 'the man in the moon']

Treasure House resources
- Vocabulary, Grammar and Punctuation Skills Pupil Book 2, Grammar Unit 3B, pages 22–23

- Collins Connect Treasure House Vocabulary, Grammar and Punctuation Year 2, Grammar Unit 3
- Photocopiable Grammar Unit 3B, Resource 1: Ice-cream noun phrases, page 91
- Photocopiable Grammar Unit 3B, Resource 2: Noun phrases to specify, page 92

Additional resources
- Groups of objects and pictures of groups of things that share the same noun

Introduction

Teaching overview

This unit introduces children to the concept of expanding noun phrases to specify exactly which thing we mean. A noun phrase is a group of words that work together and contain a noun, for example, 'the girl'. Noun phrases can be expanded with the addition of adjectives to differentiate the noun from other nouns of the same type, for example, 'the sweet little girl with blond hair and freckles' (as opposed to 'the teenage girl with the black hair and a bad attitude').

Use the content of this unit to develop actively children's oral vocabulary as well as their ability to understand and use the grammatical structures, giving particular support to children whose oral language skills are insufficiently developed. When modelling the teaching point, use your voice to show emphasis, intonation, tone, volume and natural speech patterns. This will help beginner learners to bridge the gap between spoken and written vocabulary, grammar and punctuation.

Introduce the concept

On the board write: 'ice cream for sale here' and draw a box around it, as if it were a sign in a shop. Ask for a volunteer to come to the front of the class to help you by pretending to buy an ice cream. Instruct the volunteer to ask you for an ice cream. When they ask, say: 'Which ice cream would you like?' Explain to the class that you know the volunteer would like an ice cream but unless they are more specific then you won't know which ice cream they want.

Ask all the children to suggest words or phrases that could be used to describe different ice creams and write these on the board. Then ask your original volunteer to choose some of the descriptive words to be more specific about the ice cream they would like. If they are unsure how to build the phrase, use the following example: 'I would like the vanilla double-scoop ice cream in a cone with sprinkles and chocolate sauce please!'

Pupil practice

Pupil Book pages 22–23

Get started

The children copy phrases, then find and underline the noun being specified. You may wish to support the children by reading each sentence aloud, then pausing while they find and point to the noun that is being specified, before asking them to copy the sentences.

Answers
1. the art <u>teacher</u>   [example]
2. my fluffy <u>socks</u>   [1 mark]
3. a sharp <u>pencil</u>   [1 mark]
4. the rude <u>boy</u> with the curly hair   [1 mark]
5. that <u>book</u> about hammerhead sharks   [1 mark]

Try these

The children copy and complete sentences by selecting the most appropriate words from the boxes to fill the gaps.

Answers
1. I like to wear the <u>shiny</u> shoes.   [example]
2. Mum is making the <u>cheese</u> sandwiches.   [1 mark]
3. The artist finished his <u>life-size</u> painting. [1 mark]
4. My dad drives the car <u>with the green trailer</u>.   [1 mark]
5. My friend Ali is the footballer <u>with the spiky hair</u>.   [1 mark]

Now try these

The children describe the nouns 'fish' and 'pizza' using adjectives to be more specific, then use them in sentences of their own. You may wish to support children by discussing their sentences before setting them to work independently.

Answers

1. Accept any sentences that expand the noun 'fish' with appropriate adjectives and/or descriptive prepositional or adverbial phrases, for example, 'We caught one of those big, green scaly fish last week.'
[2 marks: 1 mark for an expanded noun phrase; 1 mark for a sentence that correctly uses the expanded noun phrase]

2. Accept any sentences that expand the noun 'pizza' with appropriate adjectives and/or descriptive prepositional or adverbial phrases, for example, 'Dan prefers the pizza with the spicy sauce on it.'
[2 marks: 1 mark for an expanded noun phrase; 1 mark for a sentence that correctly uses the expanded noun phrase]

Support, embed & challenge

Support

Use Grammar Unit 3B Resource 1: Ice-cream noun phrases, to support these children in understanding the concept of being more specific by building on the ice-cream example used in the introduction. Ask the children to design their own ice-cream stall with different flavours, toppings and sizes. They write the words for these options in boxes on the worksheet. Then the children can ask their friends which ice cream they would choose. Finally, children choose three examples of specific ice-cream descriptions to write down.

Embed

Show the children pictures of two or more things that share the same noun, for example, a group of horses, a pile of shoes, a row of houses. Ask the children questions about the pictures, for example, 'Which horse looks the friendliest?' Request they answer your questions using expanded noun phrases, for example, 'the little horse with the brown legs'. You could also use related objects for this exercise, such as a selection of pens, balls and bags. Try to include and ask questions about some objects and pictures of things that are very similar, such as bags of the same colour, balls of the same size to challenge the children to be really specific and not to rely on the most obvious details such as colour and size.

Use Grammar Unit 3B Resource 2, Noun phrases to specify, to enable the children to write their own expanded noun phrases to be specific about a range of items. Ask the children to look at the questions, then write a description of the item they think of, including as much specific detail as they can. Encourage them to be creative and imaginative – answers could be silly or sensible.

Challenge

Challenge these children to write a short story about seven dwarfs. Tell them they must not refer to any of the dwarfs by name but should use noun phrases such as 'the sleepy dwarf who yawned a lot', or 'the scowling, grumpy dwarf'.

Homework / Additional activities

What happens next?

Ask the children to write three sentences about items that could be found at a party. Challenge them to describe the nouns in lots of detail, using adjectives before them and extra information after them to be specific about which objects they are talking about.

Collins Connect: Grammar Unit 3

Ask the children to complete Grammar Unit 3 (see Teach → Year 2 → Vocabulary, Grammar and Punctuation → Grammar Unit 3).

Note: the Collins Connect activities could be used with Grammar Unit 3A or 3B.

# Grammar Unit 4: Sentence types: statements

Overview

English curriculum objectives
- How the grammatical patterns in a sentence indicate its functions as a statement, question, exclamation or command

Treasure House resources
- Vocabulary, Grammar and Punctuation Skills Pupil Book 2, Grammar Unit 4, pages 24–25

- Collins Connect Treasure House Vocabulary, Grammar and Punctuation Year 2, Grammar Unit 4
- Photocopiable Grammar Unit 4, Resource 1: Is it a statement? page 93
- Photocopiable Grammar Unit 4, Resource 2: Writing statements, page 94

Additional resources
- Large detailed pictures

Introduction

Teaching overview

This unit introduces children to the concept that a sentence that tells us a fact is called a 'statement'. Statements typically follow the pattern of a subject, followed by a verb, followed by a further unit such as a direct object, and ending with a full stop, for example, 'Wendy loves her grandchildren.', 'My hair is wet.', 'He eats an apple every day.' (Statements can end with an exclamation mark, making them an exclamatory statement, but these are not included in this unit to avoid confusion with exclamations.)

Use the content of this unit to develop actively children's oral vocabulary as well as their ability to understand and use the grammatical structures, giving particular support to children whose oral language skills are insufficiently developed. When modelling the teaching point, use your voice to show emphasis, intonation, tone, volume and natural speech patterns. This will help beginner learners to bridge the gap between spoken and written vocabulary, grammar and punctuation.

Introduce the concept

Explain to the children that there are different types of sentences. In today's lesson, they will learn about statements. Say: 'Statements tell us a fact. Statements should end with a full stop.'

Write the following examples on the board: 'The earth is round.', 'The horse jumped over the fence.', 'I love eating chocolate.'

Point to the sentences and read them. Tell the children that these are statements because they each tell us a fact. Ask each child in turn to contribute a statement. If they struggle, suggest topics for them, such as what they had for breakfast, what they are wearing, what they like or don't like, who their friends are, what they will do after school. Ensure their statements are full sentences and correct them if they are not.

Pupil practice

Pupil Book pages 24–25

Get started

The children read pairs of sentences, then copy the sentence that is a statement and add a full stop. You may wish to support the children by reading the pairs of sentences aloud, then pausing while they think about which sentence in each pair is a statement before asking them to write the sentences.

Answers

1. *The cow was grazing on the green grass.* *[example]*

2. The birds were singing sweetly. [1 mark]

3. The rabbits are hopping joyfully. [1 mark]

4. The farmer was mowing the field. [1 mark]

Try these

The children put words and full stops in the correct order to make statements. If they struggle, remind them that sentences start with a capital letter, end with a full stop and that 'the' indicates a noun.

Answers

1. *The rain started to fall onto the field.* *[example]*

2. The farmer carried on mowing in the rain. [1 mark]

3. The cow stood under a tree to stay dry. [1 mark]

4. Carl has rabbits that live in a hutch. / Carl has a hutch that rabbits live in. [1 mark]

5. The mouse went back to his hole so he could keep warm. [1 mark]

Now try these

The children write a statement about two topics: something they see on the way to school and something they do in the morning. You may wish to support the children by discussing their sentences before setting them to work independently. Encourage them to think carefully about word order and to use the correct punctuation.

Answers

1. Accept any appropriate sentences that are accurately formed and punctuated as statements, for example, 'There are a lot of cars on the roads, on the way to school.' [1 mark]

2. Accept any appropriate sentences that are accurately formed and punctuated as statements, for example, 'I have breakfast and brush my teeth.' [1 mark]

Support, embed & challenge

Support

Use Grammar Unit 4 Resource 1: Is it a statement?, to support these children in learning what a statement is. Ask the children to read carefully through the phrases and sentences and tick those that are statements. Use the opportunity to discuss with the children why some of the phrases are not sentences (they don't make sense, they don't use a capital letter or full stop).

Answers

1. ✓, 2. ✗, 3. ✓, 4. ✓, 5. ✗, 6. ✓, 7. ✓, 8. ✗

Embed

Organise the children into groups and provide each group with a picture, ensuring each group only sees their own picture. Make sure there is plenty in the pictures to write about. Ask the children to work together in their groups to write statements about their pictures, for example, 'The weather is stormy.', 'A man is drinking coffee.', 'There is a cat under a chair. The cat looks scared.' Encourage the children to be observant and write about obscure details in

the pictures that are not immediately noticeable. When they have finished writing their statements, gather in the pictures and display them for everyone to see (ensure they are large enough). Ask each group to read their statements. The other groups must deduce which picture the statements describe.

Use Grammar Unit 4 Resource 2: Writing statements, to enable children to practise writing their own statements, making sure they use full sentences with the correct punctuation. First, the children should try to explain in their own words what a statement is. Then they should discuss the words listed on the resource sheet with a partner or small group and think of suitable statements to write about each item.

Challenge

Challenge the children to write three statements about a hobby they have. They could write about books they have read, things they like to draw or games they like to play. Remind them to think about word order and use the correct punctuation. Suggest that they try to include adjectives before the nouns to make the sentences more interesting.

Homework / Additional activities

What happens next?

Ask the children to write three statements about something they enjoy doing at home. They could write about places they visit, things they do and people they see. Remind them to think about word order and use the correct punctuation. Suggest that they try to use adjectives before the nouns to make the sentences interesting.

Collins Connect: Grammar Unit 4

Ask the children to complete Grammar Unit 4 (see Teach → Year 2 → Vocabulary, Grammar and Punctuation → Grammar Unit 4).

Grammar Unit 5: Sentence types: questions

Overview

English curriculum objectives

- How the grammatical patterns in a sentence indicate its functions as a statement, question, exclamation or command

Treasure House resources

- Vocabulary, Grammar and Punctuation Skills Pupil Book 2, Grammar Unit 5, pages 26–27

- Collins Connect Treasure House Vocabulary, Grammar and Punctuation Year 2, Grammar Unit 5
- Photocopiable Grammar Unit 5, Resource 1: Question words, page 95
- Photocopiable Grammar Unit 5, Resource 2: Questions, page 96

Introduction

Teaching overview

This unit builds on the previous unit looking at sentence types. This unit focuses on questions. There are two types of question: those that elicit a 'yes' or 'no' answer, for example, 'Do you like owls?', 'Will you marry me?' and those that are 'open' and can elicit any number of responses, for example, 'Who are you?', 'What do you want?', 'Where are you going?' These open-ended questions usually use a question word ('who', 'whose', 'what', 'where', 'when', 'why', 'which' and 'how') which usually (but not always) goes at the beginning of the sentence. All questions end with a question mark.

Use the content of this unit to develop actively children's oral vocabulary as well as their ability to understand and use the grammatical structures, giving particular support to children whose oral language skills are insufficiently developed. When modelling the teaching point, use your voice to show emphasis, intonation, tone, volume and natural speech patterns. This will help beginner learners to bridge the gap between spoken and written vocabulary, grammar and punctuation.

Introduce the concept

Ask the children: 'When you read, how do you know if you are reading a question?' Elicit ideas (some children may already have awareness of question marks). Establish that questions end in a question mark. Draw a question mark on the board. Explain to the children that questions are a type of sentence.

Play a game with the children. Tell the children you are thinking of a child in the class. Have all the children stand up. Ask them to guess who you are thinking of by asking you questions, such as 'Do they have blond hair?', 'Do they wear glasses?' When the children think of a question, they should raise their hand. Give them the opportunity to ask their question. Write the question on the board, emphasising the initial capital letter and question mark at the end. You could invite the child asking the question to add the question mark for you. Answer the question 'yes' or 'no'. According to your answers, those children who are eliminated sit down until the student you are thinking of is the last standing.

Tell the children that questions often use a special question word, which usually (but not always) goes at the beginning of the sentence. Establish that the purpose of a question is to ask for information. Write the question words 'why', 'what', 'where', 'how', 'who', 'which' and 'when' on the board (include others if the children suggest them). Model how to write a question by writing examples such as 'What do cows eat?' and 'How much grass is there?' on the board. Read the questions, using your voice to emphasise the question word and the rise in tone at the end.

Pupil practice

Get started

The children read pairs of sentences, then copy the sentence that is a question and add a question mark. You may wish to support the children by reading the pairs of sentences aloud, then pausing while they think about which sentence in each pair is a question before asking them to write the sentences.

Answers

1. *Was the farmer in the field?*   *[example]*

2. Where was he?   [1 mark]

3. How did he feel?   [1 mark]

4. Was there lots of work to do?   [1 mark]

Try these

The children put words in the correct order to make questions, then use a capital letter for the first word and add a question mark to the end of each question. If they struggle, tell them that most questions start with a question word such as 'where', 'what', 'how', 'when' or 'why'.

Answers

1. *Where was the cat?*   *[example]*

2. What did the sheep do?   [1 mark]

3. How many horses are in the barn?   [1 mark]

4. When did the wind start to blow?   [1 mark]

5. Why did the farmer carry on working in the cold?   [1 mark]

Now try these

The children write questions about two characters: a jolly baker and a tall teacher. Remind them to think carefully about word order and to use the correct punctuation. You may wish to support the children by discussing their sentences before setting them to work independently.

Answers

1. Accept any appropriate sentences that are accurately formed and punctuated as questions, for example, 'What is the jolly baker baking?'   [1 mark]

2. Accept any appropriate sentences that are accurately formed and punctuated as questions, for example, 'What is the name of the tall teacher?'   [1 mark]

Support, embed & challenge

Support

Use Grammar Unit 5 Resource 1: Question words, to support these children. They consider which question word is missing from each of the questions. Tell the children to use the words from the word box to fill in the gaps. They can use each word more than once. Explain that some questions will suit more than one question word. (**Answers** Accept any choices that make sense, excepting: 3. What, 6. Where)

If children need more support, read the questions to them using intonation and show them how they can test different words in the gaps until they find the one that sounds correct.

Embed

Organise the children into groups or pairs. Ask the children to take turns to think of something they know plenty about, for example, an animal, a sport, a film. The other children must work out what the thing is by asking questions, such as: 'What sort of thing is it?', 'Where does this animal live?', 'How do the players score points in this game?', 'Who stars in this film?' Tell the children that they are not allowed to ask the question (or any rephrasing of the question) 'What is it?' Write the question words 'who', 'what', 'where', 'when', 'how' and 'why' out for those children who need support and inspiration.

To make the exercise more challenging and to encourage the children to consider their choices of questions carefully, you could set a limit on the number of questions they are allowed to ask.

Use Grammar Unit 5 Resource 2: Questions, and extend children's understanding of questions. Ask them to read the first set of questions and answer them with their own answers. Then ask them to read the set of answers and, for each answer, write the question that matches it. Remind children to use a question word and question mark. (**Answers** questions for answers: 1. What time do you wake up in the morning? 2. What is your favourite game? 3. How many brothers and sisters do you have? / Do you have any brothers or sisters? 4. When is your birthday? 5. How do you help your mum?)

Challenge

Challenge these children to write a quiz for the other children. Tell them to think of topics as a group and then each choose one of the topics to write five questions on. Encourage them to choose general knowledge topics they are interested in and provide texts and/or internet access for them to research their chosen topic. Make sure they understand that they must only ask questions the other children might know the answers to and that the questions must have a right or wrong answer. Tell them to make a note of the answers when they write the questions. Hold a class quiz with these children reading out their questions to the class and with prizes for first, second and third place.

Homework / Additional activities

What happens next?

Ask the children to talk to their friends and families about questions that contain question words and use a question mark. Ask parents to help their child spot questions in books they read at home or signs they see when outside.

Challenge the children to write three questions they could ask adults about when they were younger. Remind them to think about word order and use the correct punctuation.

Collins Connect: Grammar Unit 5

Ask the children to complete Grammar Unit 5 (see Teach → Year 2 → Vocabulary, Grammar and Punctuation → Grammar Unit 5).

Grammar Unit 6: Sentence types: exclamations

Overview

English curriculum objectives

- How the grammatical patterns in a sentence indicate its functions as a statement, question, exclamation or command

Treasure House resources

- Vocabulary, Grammar and Punctuation Skills Pupil Book 2, Grammar Unit 6, pages 28–29
- Collins Connect Treasure House Vocabulary, Grammar and Punctuation Year 2, Grammar Unit 6

- Photocopiable Grammar Unit 6, Resource 1: Sorting exclamations, page 97
- Photocopiable Grammar Unit 6, Resource 2: Writing exclamations, page 98

Additional resources

- Pictures of emotional people (for example, cartoons or comic strips)

Introduction

Teaching overview

This unit builds on the previous units looking at sentence types. This unit focuses on exclamations. An exclamation is an expression of strong emotion, such as fear or surprise, or of physical pain. An exclamation mark is used at the end of an exclamation to indicate that it is to be read or interpreted with feeling.

Use the content of this unit to actively develop children's oral vocabulary as well as their ability to understand and use the grammatical structures, giving particular support to children whose oral language skills are insufficiently developed. When modelling the teaching point, use your voice to show emphasis, intonation, tone, volume and natural speech patterns. This will help beginner learners to bridge the gap between spoken and written vocabulary, grammar and punctuation.

Introduce the concept

Draw an exclamation mark on the board and ask the children if any of them know what it is or if they have seen one before in a book they have read. Elicit ideas and establish that the mark you have drawn is called an 'exclamation mark'. Tell the children that the exclamation mark is used at the end of a sentence in place of a full stop if that sentence is a special type of sentence called an 'exclamation'. Explain that exclamations are sentences that we say or read loudly or with lots of feeling. They can show anger, frustration, shock, pain, surprise or excitement. Model how to write and recognise an exclamation by writing the following examples on the board and using your voice to express feeling: 'That hurts!', 'I scored three goals today!', 'How unusual!'

Pupil practice

Pupil Book pages 28–29

Get started

The children read pairs of sentences, then copy the sentence that is an exclamation and add the exclamation mark. You may wish to support the children by reading the pairs of sentences aloud, then pausing while they think about which sentence in each pair is an exclamation before asking them to write the sentences.

Answers

1. *You broke my laptop!*   *[example]*
2. I can't believe my luck!   [1 mark]
3. You kicked me!   [1 mark]

Try these

The children put words in the correct order to make exclamations. Tell the children to use a capital letter for the first word of each exclamation and to add the exclamation mark at the end.

Answers

1. *The snow didn't stop for weeks!*   *[example]*
2. That was such a loud noise!   [1 mark]
3. It is absolutely freezing!   [1 mark]
4. My heart is racing!   [1 mark]
5. It was all just a joke!   [1 mark]

Now try these

The children write their own exclamations about a sudden, scary noise in the dark and a nice surprise. Remind the children to think carefully about what feelings their exclamations express and remind them to use the correct punctuation. You may wish to support children by discussing their sentences before setting them to work independently.

Answers

1. Accept any appropriate sentences that are accurately formed and punctuated as exclamations, for example, 'I'm so scared!'

[1 mark]

2. Accept any appropriate sentences that are accurately formed and punctuated as exclamations, for example, 'What a lovely present!'

[1 mark]

Support, embed & challenge

Support

Use Grammar Unit 6 Resource 1: Sorting exclamations, to support children in learning that exclamations can show a range of emotions. Ask the children to read the exclamations and sort them into the different categories. Extend the task by asking the children to add their own examples to each category too. (**Answers** Surprise: What a surprise! How very strange! Anger: I am so cross with you! Go away! Happiness: What fun! How wonderful! Fear: Oh no, not again! How frightening! Accept alternative interpretations if they make sense, for example, 'What a surprise!' could also express happiness if the surprise is pleasant.)

Afterwards, ask the children to choose exclamations from the resource sheet and write short stories, pieces of dialogue or draw cartoons to give the exclamation a context.

Embed

Provide the children with pictures of people looking emotional, for example, people arguing, embracing, cheering, being surprised, looking scared. (Cartoons and comic strips could be a good source for these as they are full of action and reaction and the emotions are drawn exaggeratedly. Be sure not to include any text, though.) Ask the children to look at the people in the pictures and write what they could be saying or thinking. Remind them to include exclamation marks at the ends of the exclamations they write.

Once they have written something for one picture, ask them to pass their picture on and do the same again for a new picture. Repeat the exercise a few times so that the children have an opportunity to write exclamations for a range of emotions. At the end of the exercise, ask volunteers to share their best ideas, holding up the relevant picture as they do so.

Use Grammar Unit 6 Resource 2: Writing exclamations, to enable the children to practise writing exclamations. Ask the children to imagine that they meet a monster. Discuss the emotions they would feel and what they might say and think. Make notes on the board if appropriate. Ask the children to write their speech and thoughts, using exclamations to show emotion.

Challenge

Challenge these children to write three exclamations about a storm that is so loud and fierce that it makes people feel nervous and frightened. Tell them to use the words 'suddenly', 'flash', 'crash', 'boom', 'thunder', 'lightning' and 'rain' to help them.

Homework / Additional activities

What happens next?

Ask the children to write three exclamations about a sports match (for example, football) that makes people feel excited and perhaps surprised at what happens during the match. Tell them to use the words 'suddenly', 'score', 'goal', 'cheering', 'winning' and 'losing' to help them.

Collins Connect: Grammar Unit 6

Ask the children to complete Grammar Unit 6 (see Teach → Year 2 → Vocabulary, Grammar and Punctuation → Grammar Unit 6).

Grammar Unit 7: Sentence types: commands

Overview

English curriculum objectives

- How the grammatical patterns in a sentence indicate its functions as a statement, question, exclamation or command

Treasure House resources

- Vocabulary, Grammar and Punctuation Skills Pupil Book 2, Grammar Unit 7, pages 30–31
- Collins Connect Treasure House Vocabulary, Grammar and Punctuation Year 2, Grammar Unit 7

- Photocopiable Grammar Unit 7, Resource 1: Imperative verb search, page 99
- Photocopiable Grammar Unit 7, Resource 2: Commands, page 100

Additional resources

- An instructional video or set of instructions to read out
- Symbols that symbolise commands

Introduction

Teaching overview

This unit builds on the previous unit looking at sentence types. This unit focuses on commands, which use imperative verbs, typically lack a subject and end with a full stop or exclamation mark, for example, 'Eat your vegetables.', 'Be quiet!', 'Don't press the red button.' Verbs in the imperative are always in the base (present, simple) forms of the verbs. They become imperative when they are used at or near the beginning of a command sentence. A sentence is not a command without an imperative verb.

Use the content of this unit to develop actively children's oral vocabulary as well as their ability to understand and use the grammatical structures, giving particular support to children whose oral language skills are insufficiently developed. When modelling the teaching point, use your voice to show emphasis, intonation, tone, volume and natural speech patterns. This will help beginner learners to bridge the gap between spoken and written vocabulary, grammar and punctuation.

Introduce the concept

Play a game of 'Simon says …' with the children, giving them commands to follow, such as: 'Simon says jump up and down.', 'Simon says rub your tummy.', 'Simon says clap your hands.' Invite

volunteers to give commands also. Write a set of commands on the board, such as: 'Stand up.', 'Hop on one leg.', 'Pat your head.', 'Sit down.' Write 'Simon says …' at the top of the board. Tell the children that you are going to carry on playing 'Simon says …' but that you are going to play silently. When you point to a command, they must read it and follow it. Once you have played a few times, varying the order in which you point to the commands, ask the children: 'What types of sentences are these?' Elicit that (or explain to them that) they are commands.

Read through the commands on the board again and ask the children to repeat them after you, copying your intonation and expression to make the sentences sound firm and authoritative. Explain that commands use 'bossy' words called 'imperative verbs'. Point out the imperative verbs in the commands on the board and give the children more examples, such as 'put', 'take', 'give', 'stop', 'fetch', 'get', 'tell' and 'listen', writing them on the board also.

Tell the children that the imperative verb is often at the beginning of a command. Also tell the children that commands can be as short as a single imperative verb ending with a full stop or an exclamation mark, for example, 'Stop!', 'Help!' Ensure the children know that commands are sentences, they begin with a capital letter, end in a full stop or exclamation mark, they tell the reader or listener what to do and they always contain an imperative verb.

Pupil practice

Pupil Book pages 30–31

Get started

The children copy sentences, then find and underline the imperative verbs. You may wish to support the children by reading each sentence aloud, then pausing while they find and point to the imperative verbs, before asking them to copy the sentences.

Answers

1. _Cut the paper carefully._ _[example]_

2. <u>Write</u> the date. [1 mark]

3. <u>Listen</u> to the teacher! [1 mark]

4. Now <u>change</u> your clothes for PE. [1 mark]

5. Please <u>pack</u> your bag. [1 mark]

Try these

The children copy and complete commands with a suitable imperative verb.

Answer

1. _Read your book every night._ _[example]_

2. Accept any suitable imperative verb, such as 'learn', 'practise', 'know': 'Learn your times tables.' [1 mark]

3. Accept any suitable imperative verb, such as 'bake', 'make', 'ice': 'Bake a cake for the party.' [1 mark]

4. Accept any suitable imperative verb, such as 'write', 'post', 'send': 'Please write a thank-you letter to your aunt.' [1 mark]

5. Accept any suitable imperative verb, for example, 'If you are cold, put on a warm jumper.' [1 mark]

Now try these

The children write commands for two activities: playing football and making a model. Remind them to use imperative verbs. You may wish to support children by reading the words in the sentences together before setting them to work independently.

Answers

1. Accept any appropriate sentences that are accurately formed using imperative verbs and punctuated as commands, for example, 'Pass the ball to Kieran!' [1 mark]

2. Accept any appropriate sentences that are accurately formed using imperative verbs and punctuated as commands, for example, 'Read the instructions carefully.' [2 marks]

Support, embed & challenge

Support

Use Grammar Unit 7 Resource 1: Imperative verb search, to support these children in practising recognising imperative verbs. Remind them that imperative verbs are sometimes called 'bossy' words because they tell someone to do something. Ask the children to colour in all the boxes that contain imperative verbs (verbs in their simple, present form). If they struggle, encourage them to test the word in a command sentence: '[word] the [noun]'; [word] your [noun]'. Only imperative verbs will make sense in this context, nouns and verbs in any other form will not. (**Answers** eat, fetch, pack, stop, cut, go, turn, talk, chop, fold, wait, listen, write, read, change, draw)

Embed

Watch an instructional video with the children, for example, a clip from a cooking show, a safety video, an arts and crafts or hobby tutorial. Ensure there are plenty of imperative verbs in the clip for the children to spot. (If you can't find a suitable video clip, read a set of instructions from, for example, a cookery book, device user instructions, or a flatpack furniture construction manual.) Ask the children to listen carefully and raise their hands whenever they hear an imperative verb. Pause when they raise their hands and ask them to identify the verb.

Use Grammar Unit 7 Resource 2: Commands, to enable the children to practise recalling and writing commands. Tell children to think of all the things they are asked to do each day by their family, their teacher and their friends and write them as a list of commands. Encourage children to start by thinking about when they wake up in the morning and finish when they think about going to bed at night. Some examples are provided on the resource sheet.

Provide children with images of symbols that instruct, such as the washing instructions on the labels of clothes, symbols on street signs that warn or instruct, cooking or disposal instructions on food packaging. Ensure the children understand what each symbol means. Ask the children to write a command for each symbol, such as: 'Wash at 30 degrees.', 'Watch out for pedestrians.', 'Beware of the bull.', 'Recycle this bottle.'

Challenge

Challenge these children to write three sentences giving instructions on how to do something. They could be instructions for making a sandwich or for helping with jobs at home. Ask the children to use imperative verbs and the correct punctuation.

Homework / Additional activities

What happens next?

Ask the children to write a set of instructions about how to play their favourite game. They could imagine that they are telling a child new to their school how to play the game. Ask the children to use imperative verbs and the correct punctuation.

Collins Connect: Grammar Unit 7

Ask the children to complete Grammar Unit 7 (see Teach → Year 2 → Vocabulary, Grammar and Punctuation → Grammar Unit 7).

Grammar Unit 8A: Past tense

Overview

English curriculum objectives
- Correct choice and consistent use of present tense and past tense throughout writing

Treasure House resources
- Vocabulary, Grammar and Punctuation Skills Pupil Book 2, Grammar Unit 8A, pages 32–33
- Collins Connect Treasure House Vocabulary, Grammar and Punctuation Year 2, Grammar Unit 8
- Photocopiable Grammar Unit 8A, Resource 1: Past or future tense, page 101
- Photocopiable Grammar Unit 8A, Resource 2: Yesterday, page 102

Introduction

Teaching overview

This unit focuses on understanding the past tense and using it consistently. Tense is expressed through verb forms. Verbs describe actions and we can tell when those actions take place according to how the verb has been modified. There are three main tenses: past, present and future. There are three forms of past tense: simple (for example, 'I played', 'I sang'), progressive (for example, 'I was playing', 'I was singing') and perfect (for example, 'I had played', 'I had sung'). This unit focuses on the past simple (the past progressive is covered in Unit 9). It is important that the children learn to use tenses consistently.

Use the content of this unit to actively develop children's oral vocabulary as well as their ability to understand and use the grammatical structures, giving particular support to children whose oral language skills are insufficiently developed. When modelling the teaching point, use your voice to show emphasis, intonation, tone, volume and natural speech patterns. This will help beginner learners to bridge the gap between spoken and written vocabulary, grammar and punctuation.

Introduce the concept

Ask a child: 'What did you do last night?' Encourage them to respond with a full sentence, for example, 'I watched television.', 'I did my homework.', 'I ate

dinner.' If necessary, help them to use the correct tense. Write their answer on the board and ask another child a question about past events. You could ask the same question again or, for variety, ask other questions, such as: 'What did you do at the weekend?', 'What did you have for breakfast this morning?', 'Where did you last go on holiday?' Write the children's responses on the board, ensuring they answer in full sentences in the past tense. Underline the verbs in each sentence. Explain to (or remind) the children that verbs are words that show the action in a sentence. Tell them that, in today's lesson, they will think about how to correctly use verbs in the past tense. Ask them to tell you what 'the past' means. Elicit ideas and establish that the past is what has already happened.

Read through the sentences on the board, elaborating on and explaining each example of the past tense, for example, say: 'I watched television. I am not going to watch television later. I am not watching television now. I watched television in a time before now.' Emphasise the verbs 'watched', 'to watch', and 'watching' to show the different verb forms related to different times. Discuss more examples, such as: 'I ate my dinner.', 'I tidied my room.'

Point out that most verbs in their past tense form just have '–ed' added and discuss any irregular verbs that come up, such as 'went', 'ate', 'ran', 'swam', 'heard', 'saw'.

Pupil practice

Pupil Book pages 32–33

Get started

The children copy sentences, then find and underline the verbs in the past tense. You may wish to support the children by reading each sentence aloud, then pausing while they find and point to the past tense verb, before asking them to copy the sentences.

Answers

1. I <u>lost</u> my favourite scarf.   [example]
2. Mum <u>helped</u> Grandma to move house.   [2 marks]
3. On Saturday, we <u>rode</u> our bikes to the park.   [2 marks]
4. Billy <u>shouted</u> at the football players.   [2 marks]
5. The baby <u>crawled</u> across the room.   [2 marks]

Try these

The children copy and complete sentences by choosing the past tense verbs from the boxes to fill the gaps.

Answers

1. *Yesterday we <u>walked</u> a really long way.* *[example]*

2. It <u>rained</u> all day last Sunday. [1 mark]

3. When my hamster escaped, I <u>worried</u> about it. [1 mark]

4. The baby birds <u>flew</u> out of the nest when they were ready. [1 mark]

5. We <u>slept</u> in the car because it was a long journey. [1 mark]

Now try these

The children rewrite sentences, changing them from present to past tense.

Answers

1. Nina's grandfather waited for her to come home from school. [1 mark]

2. The boy ran through the dark woods quickly. [1 mark]

Support, embed & challenge

Support

Use Grammar Unit 8A Resource 1: Past or future tense, to support these children in learning to recognise when the action in a sentence happened. Ask the children to read the sentences and then tick to show whether the sentence is describing the past or the future. Ask the children to underline the verb in each sentence to focus them on the form of the verb. (**Answers** Past: 1. I <u>swam</u> across the pool. 3. We <u>walked</u> to school this morning. 6. I <u>finished</u> my homework on Sunday. 8. I <u>opened</u> my present last night. Future: 2. I <u>will swim</u> tomorrow. 4. I <u>am going</u> to walk to school on Friday. 5. I must <u>finish</u> my homework tonight. 7. I <u>will open</u> my present in the morning.)

Embed

Compose a story as a class. Say an opening sentence that emphasises that the story is set in the past, such as: 'Once upon a time, there lived a brave little girl.', 'Long ago and far away there lived a cruel king.' Ask a child to contribute the next phrase or sentence of the story, ensuring their contribution is in the past tense. Each child, in turn, should contribute a phrase or sentence to the story, building on what the previous children have contributed. Support those who need help and beware of impatient children who try to influence other children's ideas. Ensure all contributions are in the past tense.

When each child has had their turn, recap the story, however bizarre, and give it an ending. Look back on and discuss the past tense verbs that were used, pointing out any that are irregular.

Use Grammar Unit 8A Resource 2: Yesterday, to provide the children with practise using the past tense in their writing. Ask the children to write a short diary entry about what they did yesterday. Encourage them to use the past tense verbs from the word box, although they can also use any others they like. To get them started, you may wish to discuss with them what they did yesterday before they begin to write.

Challenge

Challenge these children to write three sentences in the past tense to say what things they did when they were younger.

Homework / Additional activities

What happens next?

Ask the children to write an account of their last holiday or trip somewhere.

Collins Connect: Grammar Unit 8

Ask the children to complete Grammar Unit 8 (see Teach → Year 2 → Vocabulary, Grammar and Punctuation → Grammar Unit 8).

Note: the Collins Connect activities could be used with Grammar Unit 8A or 8B.

Grammar Unit 8B: Present tense

Overview

English curriculum objectives
- Correct choice and consistent use of present tense and past tense throughout writing

Treasure House resources
- Vocabulary, Grammar and Punctuation Skills Pupil Book 2, Grammar Unit 8B, pages 34–35

- Collins Connect Treasure House Vocabulary, Grammar and Punctuation Year 2, Grammar Unit 8
- Photocopiable Grammar Unit 8B, Resource 1: Present tense verb search, page 103
- Photocopiable Grammar Unit 8B, Resource 2: Past and present tense sentences, page 104

Introduction

Teaching overview

This unit focuses on understanding the present tense and using it consistently. Tense is expressed through verb forms. Verbs describe actions and we can tell when those actions take place according to how the verb has been modified. There are three main tenses: past, present and future. There are three forms of present tense: simple (for example, 'I play', 'I sing'), progressive (for example, 'I am playing', 'I am singing') and perfect (for example, 'I have played', 'I have sung'). This unit focuses on the present simple (the present progressive is covered in Unit 9). It is important that the children learn to use tenses consistently.

This unit introduces children to the concept of using verbs in the present tense.

Use the content of this unit to develop actively children's oral vocabulary as well as their ability to understand and use the grammatical structures, giving particular support to children whose oral language skills are insufficiently developed. When modelling the teaching point, use your voice to show emphasis, intonation, tone, volume and natural speech patterns. This will help beginner learners to bridge the gap between spoken and written vocabulary, grammar and punctuation.

Introduce the concept

Think of a thing and then describe it to the children as a riddle in the first person and present tense without

saying what that thing is. For example, you could describe a tree by saying: 'I am made of wood. I sway in the wind. I grow leaves in the spring and shed them in the autumn.' Finish with the question 'What am I?' and invite the children to guess the answer. Organise the children into pairs or groups. Ask each child to take a turn to think of a riddle for the other children. Ensure they follow the pattern demonstrated, using the first person and present tense and finishing with the question 'What am I?'

Bring the class together again. Explain to (or remind) the children that verbs are words that show the action in a sentence. Tell them that in today's lesson they will think about how to use verbs correctly in the present tense. Invite volunteers to say their riddles to the class. Write their riddles on the board and underline the present tense verbs. Ask them to tell you what 'present' means. Elicit ideas and establish that this means the action is something that happens regularly or a state that is true now.

Discuss the children's riddles on the board in more detail, for example, 'I am made of wood.' is something that is true all the time and the present tense verb is 'am'; 'I sway in the wind.' is true whenever there is wind and the present tense verb is 'sway'; 'I grow leaves in the spring and shed them in the autumn.' happens every spring and every autumn and the present tense verbs are 'grow' and 'shed'.

Pupil practice

Pupil Book pages 34–35

Get started

The children copy sentences, then find and underline the verbs in the present tense. You may wish to support the children by reading each sentence aloud, then pausing while they find and point to the verbs in the present tense, before asking them to copy the sentences.

Answers

1. I _dance_ to the music that Henry recorded. *[example]*
2. I <u>use</u> Mum's computer these days because mine broke. [1 mark]
3. She ironed the shirts that I <u>need</u> for school. [1 mark]

4. We sailed on the lake all last summer and now we <u>know</u> it well. [1 mark]

5. I <u>am</u> nervous of the dog because it bit me last week. [1 mark]

Try these

The children copy and complete sentences by choosing the present tense verbs from the boxes to fill the gaps.

Answers

1. *If I close my eyes tightly, I see bright spots.* [example]

2. Alexa cries every time she reads that book. [1 mark]

3. When I go shopping with Nan, I carry her bags. [1 mark]

4. If I chat on the phone with Sam, it's always for hours. [1 mark]

5. I always try my best to do my homework well. [1 mark]

Now try these

The children rewrite sentences, changing them from past to present tense.

Answers

1. Nina always plays at Sophie's house on Tuesday afternoons. [1 mark]

2. The boy rides his bike to school every day. [1 mark]

Support, embed & challenge

Support

Use Grammar Unit 8B Resource 1: Present tense verb search, to support children in practising recognising verbs in the present tense. Ask the children to colour in all the boxes that contain verbs in the present tense, then write how many present tense verbs they found. (**Answers** play, chat, wash, try, dance, iron, runs, laughs, sink, bite, carries, cries, see, use, sleep, rides)

Embed

Use Grammar Unit 8B Resource 2: Past and present tense sentences, to provide practice differentiating between the past and the present tense. Ask the children to read the sentences and then write 'present' or 'past' after each one according to its tense. (**Answers** 1. present, 2. present, 3. past, 4. past, 5. present, 6. past, 7. present, 8. present)

Write the following rhyme on the board and read it through with the children: 'I am a worm and I wriggle around. I wiggle on grass and I wiggle underground. I jiggle and squiggle and wiggle up and down. I am a worm and I wriggle around.' Ask the children what tense this silly rhyme is in. Confirm that it is in the present tense. Ask a volunteer to underline all the present tense verbs in the rhyme.

Ask the children to write their own silly animal rhymes using the present tense. You may wish to give them rhyming word clusters to help them, such as: 'cat', 'hat', and 'bat', 'mole', 'hole', and 'vole'. You may also wish to give them associated verb suggestions, for example, cats 'sleep', 'purr', 'bite' and 'scratch', moles 'dig', 'tunnel' and 'snuffle'. Once they have written their rhymes, ask volunteers to share their writing.

Challenge

Challenge these children to write about a hobby, club or activity that they do every week. Ask them to make sure they describe it in the present tense. Provide example verbs to support them, such as 'dance', 'ride', 'play', 'attend'.

Homework / Additional activities

What happens next?

Ask the children to write three sentences about a chore that they help out with at home every week in the present tense. Provide example verbs to support them: 'tidy', 'sort', 'fetch', 'clean', 'help'.

Collins Connect: Grammar Unit 8

Ask the children to complete Grammar Unit 8 (see Teach → Year 2 → Vocabulary, Grammar and Punctuation → Grammar Unit 8).

Note: the Collins Connect activities could be used with Grammar Unit 8A or 8B.

Grammar Unit 9: Progressive verb forms in the present tense and past tense

Overview

English curriculum objectives

- Use of the **progressive** form of **verbs** in the **present** and **past tense** to mark actions in progress [for example, 'she is drumming', 'he was shouting']

Treasure House resources

- Vocabulary, Grammar and Punctuation Skills Pupil Book 2, Grammar Unit 9, pages 36–37

- Collins Connect Treasure House Vocabulary, Grammar and Punctuation Year 2, Grammar Unit 9
- Photocopiable Grammar Unit 9, Resource 1: Sorting tenses, page 105
- Photocopiable Grammar Unit 9, Resource 2: The volcano, page 106

Additional resources

- Pairs of spot-the-difference pictures

Introduction

Teaching overview

This unit focuses on use of the progressive form of verbs in the present and past tense to mark actions in progress. Tense is expressed through verb forms. Verbs describe actions and we can tell when those actions take place according to how the verb has been modified. There are three main tenses: past, present and future. There are three forms of past tense and three forms of present tense: simple (for example, 'I played', 'I sing'), progressive (for example, 'I was playing', 'I am singing') and perfect (for example, 'I had played', 'I have sung'). This unit focuses on the past and present progressive tenses. It is important that the children learn to use tenses consistently.

Use the content of this unit to develop actively children's oral vocabulary as well as their ability to understand and use the grammatical structures, giving particular support to children whose oral language skills are insufficiently developed. When modelling the teaching point, use your voice to show emphasis, intonation, tone, volume and natural speech patterns. This will help beginner learners to bridge the gap between spoken and written vocabulary, grammar and punctuation.

Introduce the concept

Ask the children to look around them and tell you what is happening right now. Say: 'For example, I am teaching and you are learning.' Write 'I am teaching.', 'We are learning.' on the board. Listen to the children's ideas and write their suggestions on the board, ensuring they are in the present progressive tense. Make sure the children provide examples that include 'am', 'is' and 'are', prompting if necessary.

Write the sentence 'I teach.' next to the sentence 'I am teaching.' Explain to the children that the statement 'I teach.' means that teaching is something

you do, generally, in your life whereas 'I am teaching.' means you are teaching right now, as you speak; it is something that is still happening. Tell the children that this is called the 'present progressive tense'. Underline '–ing' at the end of 'teaching' and inform the children that verbs describing continuous actions all have '–ing' on the end.

Underline the '–ing' in each verb on the board. Also underline 'am', 'is' and 'are' in each sentence and explain that, in the present progressive tense, verbs ending '–ing' are used with 'am', 'is' and 'are' (present tense conjugations of the verb 'to be').

Point out that: 'am' always follows 'I'; 'is' follows 'he', 'she' and 'it'; 'are' follows 'you', 'we' and 'they'. Read through the examples on the board, emphasising and discussing the components in each sentence.

Ask the children what they were doing at a specific time in the past, for example, 'What were you all doing at six o' clock, yesterday evening?' Give them an example response, such as 'I was eating my dinner.' Write your example on the board and do the same for the children's answers. Ask more questions about what family members, pets and/or objects were doing at specific points in the past until you have a good selection of past progressive statements to work with.

Tell the children that this is the 'past progressive tense', which describes actions that continued for a time but that are over now. Underline the '–ing' at the ends of the verbs and 'was' and 'were' in each example on the board. Tell the children that, in the past progressive tense, verbs end '–ing' to describe continuous actions and are used with 'was' and 'were' (past tense conjugations of the verb 'to be') to show that they were happening in the past.

Point out that 'was' follows 'I', 'he', 'she' and 'it'; 'were' follows 'you', 'we' and 'they'. Read through the examples on the board, emphasising and discussing the components in each sentence.

Pupil practice

Pupil Book pages 36–37

Get started

The children copy sentences, then find and underline the words that make up the verb. Then they label the sentences 'present progressive' or 'past progressive'. You may wish to support the children by reading each sentence aloud, then pausing while they find and point to the words that make up the verb, before asking them to copy the sentences.

Answers

1. *Nafeesa was melting the chocolate for the cake. Past progressive* *[example]*

2. Amalia is riding her bike. Present progressive [2 marks]

3. Salma was singing a song. Past progressive [2 marks]

4. Javid was writing a letter. Past progressive [2 marks]

5. Zahir is eating a salad. Present progressive [2 marks]

Try these

The children copy and complete sentences by choosing the correct verb form from the boxes to fill the gaps.

Answers

1. *While his dad cooked, Miguel was cleaning the bathroom.* *[example]*

2. Jimi is tired so he is relaxing on the comfortable sofa. [1 mark]

3. Mum was digging the garden the whole of last weekend. [1 mark]

4. Brigitte was making silly faces at the baby and he started to cry. [1 mark]

Now try these

The children rewrite both sentences, once using the present progressive and once using the past progressive. Remind them to think carefully about how to change verbs.

1. Angela is cleaning the house. Angela was cleaning the house. [2 marks]

2. Toby is cutting up the paper. Toby was cutting up the paper. [2 marks]

Support, embed & challenge

Support

Ask these children to work in pairs and provide them with pairs of spot-the-difference pictures, one picture for each child. Ensure the pictures are full of characters doing things. The aim of the game is to spot the differences through description alone. Holding their pictures so that their partners cannot see them, the children should describe their own picture to their partner and ask questions about their partner's picture. For example, one child might say 'In my picture, a boy is riding a bike.' To which their partner might reply, 'In my picture, the boy is riding a scooter.'

Use Grammar Unit 9 Resource 1: Sorting tenses, to provide these children with practice in recognising the past and present progressive tenses. Ask the children to read the phrases and sort them into the correct column on the table. Using the examples on the resource sheet, ensure the children know to use: 'am' or 'was' with 'I'; 'is' and 'was' with 'he', 'she' and 'it'; 'are' and 'were' with 'you', 'we' and 'they'. (**Answers** Past progressive tense: were cleaning, was melting, was singing, were making, was writing, was cutting; Present progressive tense: am eating, are relaxing, is riding, are digging, is reading, is sewing)

Embed

Use Grammar Unit 9 Resource 2: The volcano, to provide the children with practise in writing in the past and present progressive tenses. Ask the children to write about life in a town situated near a volcano that has erupted. Ask the children to write sentences describing what people were doing when the volcano erupted, using the past progressive tense, for example, 'I was working in the fields when the volcano erupted.', 'The children were playing at the park when they heard the rumbling.' Then, ask the children to write sentences about what people are doing in the town now the volcano has erupted, using the present progressive tense, for example, 'My parents are building a new house.', 'We are hoping the volcano won't erupt again.'

Discuss the task together as a class before asking the children to attempt it. Invite volunteers to share what prior knowledge they might have about volcanic eruptions and help them imagine what it would be like to live near a volcano and to experience a volcanic eruption. Construct some sentences together as a group for the children to use as models for their own writing.

Challenge

Ask these children to write a paragraph that sets the scene for a story. If they have completed Grammar Unit 9 Resource 2, they could build on what they have already written and set the scene for a story about the day a volcano erupts near a town.

Alternatively, you could give them a new subject or allow them to choose a subject for themselves. Challenge them to include as many past progressive tense phrases as they can, such as: 'the birds were singing', 'the sun was shining', 'the crops were growing', 'the children were playing'.

Homework / Additional activities

What happens next?

Ask the children to write three sentences about things they were doing yesterday using the past progressive tense, for example, 'I was playing football.', 'I was taking my spelling test.', 'I was playing with my brother.'

Collins Connect: Grammar Unit 9

Ask the children to complete Grammar Unit 9 (see Teach → Year 2 → Vocabulary, Grammar and Punctuation → Grammar Unit 9).

Review unit 2: Grammar

A. Children put the words in the correct order to make sentences using 'and', 'or' and 'but'.

1. We could eat beans or we could eat peas. [1 mark]

2. I went to school and I saw my friend. [1 mark]

3. Tamir likes red but he doesn't like green. / Tamir likes green but he doesn't like red. [1 mark]

B. Children copy and complete the sentences using 'because', 'if', 'when' and 'that'.

1. I will be sad if my team loses the match. [1 mark]

2. Mum has gone shopping because it is Dad's birthday. [1 mark]

3. Dev told me that we are invited to a disco. [1 mark]

4. It might snow in England when it is winter. [1 mark]

C. Children copy and complete each sentence. They think of an adjective to fill each gap.

1. I like to eat that _____ cereal. [1 mark]

2. We splashed in the _____ puddles. [1 mark]

3. The goldfish swam round their _____ bowl. [1 mark]

D. Children copy each sentence and label it with either: 'statement', 'question', 'exclamation' or 'command'.

1. How many owls can you hear (question) [1 mark]

2. Pass me the colouring pencils (command) [1 mark]

3. We went to the cinema on Saturday morning (statement) [1 mark]

4. Wow, that's amazing (exclamation) [1 mark]

E. Children copy and complete each sentence by choosing the correct verb tense from the box.

1. Yesterday we baked some banana muffins. [1 mark]

2. Tina and I like to skip to school every morning. [1 mark]

3. Earlier today, we all listened carefully in assembly. [1 mark]

F. Children copy and complete each sentence by choosing the correct verb form from the box.

1. While his favourite act performed, Dan was cheering at the TV. [1 mark]

2. Henry is hungry so he is eating his dinner now. [1 mark]

3. Last night, Gia was knitting for hours to get the scarf finished. [1 mark]

Punctuation Unit A:
Punctuation marks

Overview

English curriculum objectives
- Use of capital letters, full stops, question marks and exclamation marks to demarcate **sentences**

Treasure House resources
- Vocabulary, Grammar and Punctuation Skills Pupil Book 2, Punctuation Unit A, pages 40–41

- Photocopiable Punctuation Unit A, Resource 1: Correcting sentences, page 107
- Photocopiable Punctuation Unit A, Resource 2: Writing sentences, page 108

Additional resources
- Blank cards

Introduction

Teaching overview

This unit focuses on sentence punctuation. Punctuation is used to structure and organise sentences, clarifying how the sentence should be read. A capital letter should always be used to indicate the beginning of a sentence. In most cases, a full stop is used to indicate the completion of a sentence. If the sentence is a question, it must always be completed with a question mark. A question mark should never be used for a sentence that is not syntactically a question (even if a question is implied).

An exclamation mark can be used in place of a full stop to indicate to the reader that the sentence should be read with emotion.

The children should have been introduced to capital letters, full stops, question marks and exclamation marks to demarcate sentences in Year 1. This year's grammar units on sentence types (see Grammar Units 4–7) should increase the children's understanding of sentence structures and end punctuation. This unit aims to continue building the children's proficiency with using capital letters, full stops, question marks and exclamation marks to punctuate sentences.

Use the content of this unit to develop actively the children's oral vocabulary as well as their ability to understand and use the grammatical structures, giving particular support to children whose oral language skills are insufficiently developed. When modelling the teaching point, use your voice to show emphasis, intonation, tone, volume and natural speech patterns. This will help beginner learners to bridge the gap between spoken and written vocabulary, grammar and punctuation.

Introduce the concept

Ask the children to remind you what types of punctuation are needed for sentences. It is likely that many of them will know about capital letters and end punctuation but this is a good opportunity to draw all

of their knowledge together to consolidate, embed and reinforce the teaching point to those that struggle to remember.

Establish that all sentences need to start with a capital letter and that all sentences must end with either a full stop, a question mark or an exclamation mark, depending on the type of sentence. Tell the children that, although they may know these points now, many children forget to apply them when they get into the flow of writing longer texts so it is important to practise and embed them as good habits as early as possible.

Write the following sentences on the board without capital letters or end punctuation and invite volunteers to correct them for you: 'london is a busy city', 'is London a busy city', 'we nearly got lost in London'.

Write: 'i can't find my fizzy drink can you find it for me'. Tell the children that you have written two sentences but you haven't used punctuation. Read the words, avoiding any intonation that implies where the sentence break should go. Ask the children what punctuation they think you should add. Take their suggestions and then show them the two possibilities: 'I can't find my fizzy drink. Can you find it for me?' and 'I can't find my fizzy drink can. You find it for me!' Discuss how, thanks to different sentence punctuation, the two possibilities have different meanings.

Write: 'The caterpillar ate a whole field of cabbages minutes after she was sick.' Discuss how this must be a very greedy caterpillar to eat that much after being sick. Tell the children that this could mean something different if it were two sentences. Write: 'The caterpillar ate a whole field of cabbages. Minutes after, she was sick.' Read these sentences and discuss how the meaning has changed.

Impress on the children the importance of demarcating their sentences using capital letters at the beginning and correct end punctuation if they want to make sense and avoid writing things they don't mean.

Pupil practice

Pupil Book pages 40–41

Get started

The children assess whether sentences have been correctly punctuated. You may wish to support the children by reading each sentence aloud, then pausing while they discuss and decide if it has correct punctuation.

Answers

1. *correct*   *[example]*

2. incorrect   [1 mark]

3. incorrect   [1 mark]

4. correct   [1 mark]

5. incorrect   [1 mark]

Try these

The children copy unpunctuated sentences and add the correct punctuation.

Answers

1. *It took me all day to tidy my bedroom.*   *[example]*

2. On Saturday, my aunt May came to visit.   [1 mark]

3. The house is on fire.   [1 mark]

4. Did you watch the big race on Sunday?   [1 mark]

5. What is the weather like today?   [1 mark]

Also accept exclamation marks as end of sentence punctuation for sentences 1, 2 and 3.

Now try these

The children compose six sentences, a sentence with a full stop, a sentence with a question mark and a sentence with an exclamation mark for each of two topics: 'party' and 'kangaroo'.

1. Accept three correctly punctuated sentences, one with a full stop, one with an exclamation mark and one question, on the subject of 'party'.

[3 marks: 1 mark per sentence]

2. Accept three correctly punctuated sentences, one with a full stop, one with an exclamation mark and one question, on the subject of 'kangaroo'.

[3 marks: 1 mark per sentence]

Support, embed & challenge

Support

Use Punctuation Unit A Resource 1: Correcting sentences, to give these children the opportunity to consolidate their knowledge of correct sentence punctuation. Ask the children to correct the sentences. They need to add capital letters at the beginning and anywhere else they think they are needed, and then add suitable end punctuation. You may need to revise examples of when capital letters are required. (**Answers** 1. Daisy and Joe went on the bus to visit their nan in Devon. 2. The teachers found a lolly stuck to the head teacher's chair. 3. The bird ate a worm and splashed in the bird bath. 4. Pascal met Jeremy and then watched Rovers FC play in the final. 5. Edwina was so hungry she thought she might faint. 6. The hall was full of people who had come to listen to the talk. 7. Gemma ordered an English breakfast with all the extras. 8. Is Verity really moving house tomorrow? Accept exclamation marks in place of full stops on any sentence, excepting 8.)

Embed

Provide each child with three pieces of blank card. Ask them to draw a full stop on one piece of card, a question mark on another and an exclamation mark on the third.

Say sentences to the class, ensuring a variety of statements, questions, exclamations and commands. Use expression and intonation to define the difference between statements and exclamations. For each sentence, have the children hold up the card with the punctuation mark they think should go at the end. Confirm the correct choice of end punctuation. You could make the game competitive by awarding one point for each correct punctuation selection and see who has the most points at the end.

Use Punctuation Unit A Resource 2: Writing sentences, to enable the children to practise independently writing correctly punctuated sentences. The resource sheet suggests different topics for the children to write about.

Challenge

Challenge these children to write correctly punctuated sentences about a book they have recently read.

Homework / Additional activities

What happens next?

Ask the children to make a poster that could be displayed in the classroom about how to correctly punctuate sentences.

Punctuation Unit 1: Commas in lists

Overview

English curriculum objectives
- Commas to separate items in a list

Treasure House resources
- Vocabulary, Grammar and Punctuation Skills Pupil Book 2, Punctuation Unit 1, pages 42–43
- Collins Connect Treasure House Vocabulary, Grammar and Punctuation Year 2, Punctuation Unit 1

- Photocopiable Punctuation Unit 1, Resource 1: Adding commas to sentences, page 109
- Photocopiable Punctuation Unit 1, Resource 2: Making lists, page 110

Additional resources
- Objects for the children to describe

Introduction

Teaching overview

A comma marks a pause or break between parts of a sentence, making the meaning clear to the reader by grouping and separating words, phrases and clauses. This unit focuses on using commas to separate items in lists. A list can be defined as three or more items. Commas should separate each item except the final two, which should be separated by the word 'and' rather than a comma. (The serial or 'Oxford' comma, the practice of using a comma before the final 'and' as well, need not be taught until Year 5 when the children will learn about using commas to avoid ambiguity.) It is often crucial to the meaning of a sentence that listed items be grouped and separated correctly. Misused or omitted commas can result (sometimes hilariously) in much ambiguity and confusion.

Use the content of this unit to develop actively children's oral vocabulary as well as their ability to understand and use the grammatical structures, giving particular support to children whose oral language skills are insufficiently developed. When modelling the teaching point, use your voice to show emphasis, intonation, tone, volume and natural speech patterns. This will help beginner learners to bridge the gap between spoken and written vocabulary, grammar and punctuation.

Introduce the concept

On the board, write: 'I enjoy running. I enjoy swimming. I enjoy climbing. I enjoy dancing.' Read the statements with the children and point out that repeating 'I enjoy' takes a long time and sounds clumsy. Tell the children that this could be written as one sentence, rather than four. Write: 'I enjoy running and swimming and climbing and dancing.' Read the

sentence through with the children and point out that there is still a lot of repetition. Tell the children that 'and' can be replaced with a punctuation mark called a 'comma'.

Model how to draw the shape of a comma and where it sits on a writing line as many children find these things difficult. Tell the children that you are not going to replace the last 'and' with a comma as it signals the end of the list. Write: 'I enjoy running, swimming, climbing and dancing.' Agree that this is the best version.

Ask volunteers to give you lists of three or more items, such as their pets' names, their favourite colours or foods they dislike the most. Write their lists on the board as sentences, omitting the commas and 'and', for example, 'The names of my pets are Harry Rover Bella.', 'My favourite colours are blue red yellow purple.' Invite the volunteers to add the commas and 'and' to the sentences.

Write: 'My favourite pizza toppings are ham and mushroom mushroom pepperoni and tomatoes and cheese and tomato.' Say: 'This is a very complicated list. I can't tell what goes with what so I'm going to try to put some commas in.' Demonstrate putting commas in the wrong places to create nonsensical toppings such as 'mushroom pepperoni', 'ham and mushroom mushroom' or 'tomatoes and cheese and tomatoes'. Take suggestions from the children and, finally, put the commas in the correct places: 'My favourite pizza toppings are ham and mushroom, mushroom, pepperoni and tomatoes, and cheese and tomato.'

Conclude that commas are useful for both grouping and separating items in lists, making the lists easier to read and less confusing.

Pupil practice

Pupil Book pages 42–43

Get started

The children look at the sentences and assess whether the commas in them have been used correctly. Suggest children write numbers 1–5 in their books. If the commas are correct, they label the sentence 'correct'. If the commas are incorrect, they label the sentence 'incorrect'. You may wish to support the children by reading each sentence aloud, then pausing while they discuss and assess the use of commas, before asking them to copy the sentences. Afterwards, ask the children to correct and write out the sentences with incorrect punctuation.

Answers

1. *Dad asked me to tidy up dust polish and vacuum the carpet. Incorrect*   *[example]*

   Dad asked me to tidy up, dust, polish and vacuum the carpet

2. I went to the park, the shop, the garage and the bank. Correct   [2 marks]

3. I saw monkeys, giraffes, elephants and hippos. Correct   [2 marks]

4. I am wearing trousers, a shirt a jumper and a tie. Incorrect   [2 marks]

   I am wearing trousers, a shirt, a jumper and a tie.

5. I play netball, football, cricket, and rounders. Incorrect   [2 marks]

   I play netball, football, cricket and rounders.

Try these

The children copy and complete sentences by adding the correct punctuation.

Answers

1. *I would like to go to France, America, Spain and Germany.*   *[example]*

2. My school bag is red, yellow, orange and pink.   [1 mark]

3. I played with Fern, Sita, Henri and Morgan.   [1 mark]

4. We have kittens, fish, gerbils and hamsters as pets.   [1 mark]

5. I have spelling, reading, Art and Maths for homework.   [1 mark]

Now try these

The children copy the sentences starters 'The people in my family are …' and 'The places I would like to visit are …' and complete sentences with their own lists.

Answers

1. Accept any appropriate and correctly punctuated lists, for example, 'The people in my family are Mum, Dad, my brother and me.'

   [3 marks: Award marks for content, correct use of commas and correct use of 'and'.]

2. Accept any appropriate and correctly punctuated lists, for example, 'The places I would like to visit are Australia, Britain, Egypt and Brazil.'

   [3 marks: Award marks for content, correct use of commas and correct use of 'and'.]

Support, embed & challenge

Support

Use Punctuation Unit 1 Resource 1: Adding commas to sentences, to provide practice in reading lists with commas and recognising where the commas should be placed in lists. Ask the children to read each sentence carefully and add commas in the correct places. (**Answers** 1. We saw sharks, stingrays, turtles, crabs, otters and jellyfish at the aquarium. 2. We bought carrots, potatoes, turnips, cauliflower, broccoli and cabbage at the supermarket. 3. I play with Maise, Malika, Joe, Scott, Tara and Dana at school. 4. I have my bed, wardrobe, drawers, desk, clothes, TV and alarm clock in my room. 5. We planted daisies, daffodils, pansies, tulips and roses in the garden. 6. I have pens, pencils, a ruler, sharpener, eraser and some stickers in my pencil case.)

Embed

Write: 'The things I love include cooking my family and my cats.' Agree that this is an alarming statement. Ask how adding a single comma could make this statement less scary. Elicit that the statement should (hopefully) read 'The things I love include cooking, my family and my cats.'

Write: 'No eating children or pets allowed.' Agree that eating children and pets shouldn't be allowed but that the sentence should probably read: 'No eating, children or pets allowed.'

Write: 'This toilet is only for people who are pregnant elderly children.' Ask what is wrong with this sentence. Elicit that pregnant elderly children don't exist so they are unlikely to have a toilet reserved for them. Confirm that the list should read 'pregnant, elderly or children.'

Write: 'Salad ingredients: tomatoes, cucumber, goats, cheese, olives and red onion.' Ask the children what is wrong with this list. Agree that nobody puts whole goats in salads and that the comma after 'goats' is a comma too many. (You may also wish to add the possessive apostrophe to 'goats'.)

Use Punctuation Unit 1 Resource 2: Making lists, to enable children to develop the ability to write their own lists, correctly punctuated with commas between the items. Ask the children to write a list for each given topic with commas used correctly between the items.

Challenge

Provide these children with objects that have numerous attributes that could be described. Challenge these children to write a sentence to describe each object using as many adjectives as they can, for example, 'The ball is big, shiny, yellow and bouncy.', 'The teddy is cute, cuddly, soft and fluffy.' You may wish to provide these children with lists of applicable adjectives to help them. If you wish to challenge them further, you could suggest they expand the noun phrases to cram even more description into their sentences, for example, 'The worn, old teddy is cute, cuddly, soft and fluffy.'

Homework / Additional activities

What happens next?

Ask the children to write lists of things at home. Things they could write lists of could include what they eat, drink, do during the day, watch on television, have in the house, want for their birthday or for Christmas, names of pets, friends or family members, and hobbies and interests.

Collins Connect: Punctuation Unit 1

Ask the children to complete Punctuation Unit 1 (see Teach → Year 2 → Vocabulary, Grammar and Punctuation → Punctuation Unit 1).

Punctuation Unit 2:
Apostrophes for omission

Overview

English curriculum objectives
- Apostrophes to mark where letters are missing in spelling and to mark singular possession in nouns [for example, 'the girl's name']

Treasure House resources
- Vocabulary, Grammar and Punctuation Skills Pupil Book 2, Punctuation Unit 2, pages 44–45

- Collins Connect Treasure House Vocabulary, Grammar and Punctuation Year 2, Punctuation Unit 2
- Photocopiable Punctuation Unit 2, Resource 1: Matching contractions to whole words, page 111
- Photocopiable Punctuation Unit 2, Resource 2: Writing contractions, page 112

Additional resources
- Things to use as buzzers (optional)

Introduction

Teaching overview

This unit focuses on using apostrophes to show omissions in contracted forms of two words. Many words that appear frequently as a pair are merged into a single word by conjoining the two words and omitting letters, for example, 'do not' becomes 'don't', 'is not' becomes 'isn't', 'he is' becomes 'he's'. These are called 'contracted words' or 'contractions'. Apostrophes are used to indicate the omitted letters.

Contractions are very common in both spoken and written English, so the children are likely to be familiar with them and will probably have some confidence using them when speaking. They are unlikely to be as confident with writing them and putting the apostrophe in the right place. They also need to be able to identify which words the contractions comprise and when it is or is not appropriate to use a contraction.

Use the content of this unit to develop actively children's oral vocabulary as well as their ability to understand and use the grammatical structures, giving particular support to children whose oral language skills are insufficiently developed. When

modelling the teaching point, use your voice to show emphasis, intonation, tone, volume and natural speech patterns. This will help beginner learners to bridge the gap between spoken and written vocabulary, grammar and punctuation.

Introduce the concept

On the board write 'aren't' and 'you're'. Ask the children if they know what the words mean and why they have punctuation marks in the middle of them. Elicit ideas and then explain that the punctuation marks are called 'apostrophes'. Tell the children that we can use an apostrophe to show omission. Explain that 'omission' means letters that have been left out. Tell the children that, when we use an apostrophe to show omission, we write two words as one word; this is shorter and more informal than writing two whole words. Model that this also reflects the way we speak in a more informal way, contrasting the formality and informality of phrases such as: 'you are alright' and 'you're alright'; 'I cannot do it' and 'I can't do it'; 'I do not know' and 'I don't know'. Show on the board that the words 'are not' can be written as 'aren't' and the words 'you are' can be written as 'you're'.

Pupil practice
Pupil Book pages 44–45

Get started

The children copy sentences, then find and underline the words that have been abbreviated. You may wish to support the children by reading each sentence aloud, then pausing while they find and point to the words that have been abbreviated, before asking them to copy the sentences.

Answers
1. *I'm late!*   *[example]*
2. We're going to the park.   [1 mark]
3. She's doing a great job.   [1 mark]
4. You shouldn't talk during a test.   [1 mark]
5. I hadn't thought about that.   [1 mark]

Try these

The children match contractions to the equivalent whole words.

Answers

1. *he's*	**d)** *he is*	*[example]*
2. they'd	**c)** they had	[1 mark]
3. wasn't	**a)** was not	[1 mark]
4. they've	**e)** they have	[1 mark]
5. couldn't	**b)** could not	[1 mark]

Now try these

The children rewrite sentences using apostrophes to contract the underlined words.

Answers

1. She's a talented dancer.	[1 mark]
2. We'd better hurry up.	[1 mark]

Support, embed & challenge

Support

Use Punctuation Unit 2 Resource 1: Matching contractions to whole words, to provide practice recognising and matching contractions to their whole-word equivalents. Ask the children to cut out the words. They can then either match them together and stick them on a piece of paper, or the cards can be used to play matching games like 'Snap!' by matching together the cards that show the shortened and whole-words versions. (**Answers** pairs: should not, shouldn't; we are, we're; I am, I'm; was not, wasn't; had not, hadn't; he is, he's; we've, we have; they are, they're; she will, she'll; we will, we'll; did not, didn't; can not, can't)

Embed

Choose eight children to sit on two quiz teams of four children each. Provide each team with something to write on and a pen. Give each team member something to use as a buzzer, such as an actual buzzer, a cow bell, a glockenspiel or noises or words such as 'bing' and 'bong'. Ensure the two teams' 'buzzers' are distinguishable.

Begin with a quick-fire round. Say two words that can be contracted. The first child to buzz in must say the contraction and then spell it, making sure to specify the position of the apostrophe. If they get it right, their team gets to answer three more questions on which they are allowed to confer. Vary the form of these questions, for example, 'What two words is "won't" a contraction of?', 'Spell the word "haven't" on your whiteboard.', 'What two letters does the apostrophe stand for in the word "I'd"?' Any questions not answered or answered incorrectly should be asked to the other team. If neither team can answer a question, a volunteer from the rest of the class (or 'audience') should be given the opportunity to answer.

Award one point for each correct answer. Keep score and, after a few rounds, announce a winning team. Form a new team of children who have not played yet to play against the winning team. Repeat the process until all the children in the class have played on a team.

Use Punctuation Unit 2 Resource 2: Writing contractions, to provide the children with practice writing whole words that match the contracted versions. Discuss the missing letters with the children and check carefully that they are placing the apostrophes in the correct places.

Answers

Whole words: she is, are not, you are, they are, will not, do not, I will, would not, has not; Contractions: didn't, he'll, he'd, it's, isn't, I'd, they'll, what's, who's

Challenge

Challenge these children to search texts for words that use apostrophes for omission. Ask them to change these words back into the whole words that make them up. Ask them how the tone of the writing changes.

Homework / Additional activities

What happens next?

Ask the children to find as many examples as they can of apostrophes used for omission.

Collins Connect: Punctuation Unit 2

Ask the children to complete Punctuation Unit 2 (see Teach → Year 2 → Vocabulary, Grammar and Punctuation → Punctuation Unit 2).

Punctuation Unit 3:
Apostrophes for possession

Introduction

Teaching overview

This unit focuses on using an apostrophe to show singular possession in nouns. To indicate that a noun has possession of something, add an apostrophe and an 's' to the noun, for example, to refer to a bucket owned by Jill, write 'Jill's bucket' or to write about the end of a journey, write 'journey's end'. The children may be confused by nouns that end in 's' or 'ss'. However, emphasise that the rule remains the same, for example, 'the boss's husband' or 'James's shirt'. The children may also be tempted to place apostrophes before the 's' at the ends of plural nouns, for example, 'egg's' when they mean 'eggs' or 'Sunday's' when they mean 'Sundays'. In this case, emphasise that there is no need for an apostrophe unless the noun owns something.

Use the content of this unit to develop actively children's oral vocabulary as well as their ability to understand and use the grammatical structures, giving particular support to children whose oral language skills are insufficiently developed. When modelling the teaching point, use your voice to show emphasis, intonation, tone, volume and natural speech patterns. This will help beginner learners to bridge the gap between spoken and written vocabulary, grammar and punctuation.

Introduce the concept

Write 'Luke's shoes' and 'the dog's bowl' on the board. Ask the children if they know why the words have punctuation marks before the letter 's'. Elicit ideas then explain that the punctuation marks are called 'apostrophes'. Tell the children that we can use an apostrophe to show possession. Explain that 'possession' means when something belongs to something or someone. Point to the examples you have written and explain that the shoes belong to Luke and the bowl belongs to the dog. Say: 'To indicate that a noun has possession of something, add an apostrophe and an "s" to the noun.'

Walk around the room, touching, picking up or pointing to things that belong to the children or to other things and ask who or what they belong to, for example, 'Whose jumper is this?', 'What are these the legs of?' Take answers from one child at a time, requiring that they write their answer on the board, for example, 'That's Sacha's jumper.', 'They are the table's legs.' Support the children in placing the apostrophe in the correct place. Utilise children's names that end in 's' to demonstrate that the rule remains the same, for example, 'Jess's ruler', 'James's bag.'

Write: 'I play football on Sundays. We won this Sundays match.' Tell the children that one of the 'Sundays' needs an apostrophe and invite them to tell you which one. Confirm that the apostrophe is missing from the second 'Sundays'. Ensure the children understand that, in the first sentence, there are lots of Sundays so 'Sunday' does need an 's' on the end. But, the Sundays don't own anything so they mustn't add an apostrophe. In the second sentence, however, there is only one Sunday being written about but the match belonged to Sunday so it needs an apostrophe and an 's' on the end.

Repeat the activity with more examples, such as: 'All the eggs smelled bad but the biggest eggs smell was the worst.', 'For breakfast, I had beans on toast and a fried hens egg.', 'One kittens sneeze made all the other kittens jump.'

Pupil practice

Pupil Book pages 46–47

Get started

The children copy sentences, then find and underline the name of the person who owns something. You may wish to support the children by reading each sentence aloud, then pausing while they find and point to the name of the person who owns something, before asking them to copy the sentences.

Answers

1. *Marie's book was full of drawings.*   *[example]*
2. I like <u>Zayn's</u> new toy.   [1 mark]
3. <u>Roger's</u> bike is bright red.   [1 mark]
4. This is <u>Denise's</u> cardigan.   [1 mark]
5. Niccolo played with <u>Dylan's</u> baking set.   [1 mark]

Try these

The children copy and complete sentences by adding apostrophes to the underlined words.

Answers

1. *Martia's bag is blue.*   *[example]*
2. The <u>dog's</u> ears are black and white.   [1 mark]
3. I used <u>Matteo's</u> new pen.   [1 mark]
4. Mike is reading <u>Tristan's</u> book about sharks.   [1 mark]
5. Has anyone seen one of <u>Grace's</u> orange trainers?   [1 mark]

Now try these

The children rewrite phrases, simplifying them by using an apostrophe. You may wish to support children by discussing the task before setting them to work independently or in pairs.

Answers

1. *the cat's blanket*   *[example]*
2. Miguel's pen   [1 mark]
3. Lily's Maths homework   [1 mark]

Support, embed & challenge

Support

Use Punctuation Unit 3 Resource 1: Showing possession, to familiarise these children with using apostrophes to indicate possession. Ask the children to look at the example on the resource sheet. Show them how to read the owner, then the object they own and how to put these together with an apostrophe and letter 's'. (**Answers** Zahid's pen, Maria's computer, Sophie's ball, Gregory's bag, Nick's book, Matt's hat, Amy's scooter)

Embed

Show the children a slideshow of real-life signs where apostrophes are either missing or have been added where they shouldn't be (there are many of these images available on the internet). Discuss with the children what is wrong with the punctuation on each sign and invite volunteers to correct it.

Use Punctuation Unit 3 Resource 2: Using possessive apostrophes, to give the children practice using possessive apostrophes by writing their own sentences. Ask the children to think of sentences they could write about the things the people own. (**Answers** 1. *Paul borrowed Sarah's toaster. [example]* 2. any sentence about 'Mrs Jones's car', 3. any sentence about 'Mr Sanchez's slippers', 4. any sentence about Chantelle's calculator, 5. any sentence about 'Joshua's book', 6. any sentence about a friend's bike, referring to the friend as 'friend' or by name, 7. any sentence about 'the squirrel's nuts', 8. any sentence about 'the bird's nest')

Challenge

Challenge these children to write a silly, short story about a collector. They could be a collector of anything and/or everything. Remind them to use apostrophes to indicate ownership.

Homework / Additional activities

What happens next?

Ask the children to find examples of possessive apostrophes in the things they read and in signs and advertisements. Ask them to copy down at least three examples to share with the class. Ask them to look out for apostrophes that have been misused and, if they spot any, write them down as a separate list and make a note of why they think the writer made a mistake.

Collins Connect: Punctuation Unit 3

Ask the children to complete Punctuation Unit 3 (see Teach → Year 2 → Vocabulary, Grammar and Punctuation → Punctuation Unit 3).

Review unit 3: Punctuation

Pupil Book pages 48–49

A. The children copy and correct the sentences by adding the correct punctuation.

a) Please may I have a cookie? [1 mark]

b) Look out – there is a car coming! [1 mark]

c) Dad helped Miguel finish his homework. [1 mark]

d) Can we take the dog for a walk? [1 mark]

e) I think it is going to rain today. [1 mark]

B. The children copy the sentences and add commas to separate the items in each list.

a) I like books about sharks, reptiles, aircraft and space. [2 marks]

b) We have potatoes, tuna, sweetcorn and salad for dinner. [2 marks]

c) My aunt, uncle, cousins and grandma are coming to visit. [2 marks]

d) I have a rubber, ruler, pencils and pens in my pencil case. [2 marks]

e) I am growing sunflowers, pumpkins, beans and strawberries in my garden. [2 marks]

C. The children match the shortened words to the whole words.

1. c)

2. d)

3. e)

4. a)

5. b)

D. The children copy and complete the sentences by adding apostrophes to the underlined words.

a) Gregory's new lunchbox has a picture of a lizard on the front. [1 mark]

b) The children left Sara's football in the playground. [1 mark]

c) Ethan's dad bought him a remote controlled helicopter. [1 mark]

d) Everyone wants a turn on Jane's scooter. [1 mark]

e) Steven found Mohammed's bookmark on the floor. [1 mark]

–ness words word search

Can you find all the words ending **–ness** in this word search?

f	o	r	g	i	v	e	n	e	s	s	d
r	a	u	n	e	u	l	e	v	t	j	k
e	h	d	q	f	r	y	w	c	u	v	b
s	m	e	r	b	j	s	n	g	b	o	d
h	l	n	k	x	m	d	e	o	b	w	a
n	w	e	t	n	e	s	s	t	o	x	r
e	g	s	h	y	n	e	s	s	r	i	k
s	p	s	e	t	q	n	h	c	n	w	n
s	l	a	t	e	n	e	s	s	n	z	e
s	u	i	a	w	a	r	e	n	e	s	s
c	o	r	r	e	c	t	n	e	s	s	s
c	a	l	m	n	e	s	s	a	s	f	p

Words to find

awareness	calmness	correctness	darkness
forgiveness	freshness	lateness	newness
rudeness	shyness	stubbornness	wetness

Can you explain what each word means?

Vocabulary Unit 1 Resource 2

–ness word sentences

Complete the sentences by using the words from the box.

braveness	cheerfulness	lateness	smoothness	weakness

1. The teacher watched the clock as she did not like _____.

2. Karen ran her hands over the _____ of the new book cover.

3. The football team's _____ was their injured goalie.

4. Tim was given a medal for his _____ when defeating the dragon.

5. Sabrina was surprised at Gran's _____ despite getting wet in the rain.

Can you make your own sentences using these **–ness** words?

forgiveness	forgetfulness	stubbornness	firmness	tiredness

1. _____

2. _____

3. _____

4. _____

5. _____

Making compound nouns

Match the words together to make compound nouns.
How many can you find?

man	toy	bag	bow
ball	glasses	tooth	snow
hand	paste	post	news
rain	paper	box	sun

Compound nouns

_____ _____

_____ _____

_____ _____

_____ _____

Do you know any other compound nouns? Write them here.

_____

_____

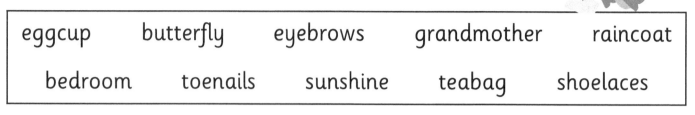

Compound noun definitions

Match the compound nouns to their definitions.

eggcup	butterfly	eyebrows	grandmother	raincoat
bedroom	toenails	sunshine	teabag	shoelaces

1. This is a place where you sleep at night. _____

2. You have two of these on your face. _____

3. These are helpful if you want your shoes to stay on your feet. _____

4. You might have this on your plate next to your toast soldiers. _____

5. This lady is your mum or dad's mum. _____

6. A beautiful insect that transforms from a caterpillar. _____

7. Keep these cut short if you don't want to scratch yourself. _____

8. A beautiful summer's day will be full of this. _____

9. Wear one of these if you want to keep dry. _____

10. Use this to brew a hot drink that gives you energy. _____

–ful and –less words crossword

Solve the clues and write the words in the crossword.

Across

1. Tara was t_____ful for her gift.

2. After watching the sad film, Mum was t_____ful.

3. That broken arm looks p_____ful.

4. Old cardboard boxes are always u_____ful.

5. The assembly went on forever, it seemed e_____less.

6. We all scored highly and were s_____ful in our tests.

Down

7. George likes to lend a hand. He is so h_____ful.

8. Dylan is brave. He is totally f_____less.

9. After running around the field I was b_____less.

10. Our new puppy is very p_____ful.

© HarperCollins*Publishers* 2017

79

–ful and –less word sentences

Read the sentences. Choose the correct words to fill the gaps.

1. The broken remote control was now _____.
   (useful / useless)

2. Dan always thinks of others. His mum says he is _____.
   (thoughtful / thoughtless)

3. The superhero had lost his powers. Now he was _____.
   (powerful / powerless)

4. Tina thinks the bus might be on time today. She feels _____.   (hopeful / hopeless)

5. My dad can't sing. His singing is _____.
   (tuneful / tuneless)

6. I would like a new, bright and _____ pencil case.
   (colourful / colourless)

7. Ravi dropped his phone because he was being _____.
   (careful / careless)

8. I was relieved that the injection was _____.
   (painful / painless)

Adverb word sums

Put the parts of the words together and write the words.
One has been done for you.

1. slow + –ly = <u>slowly</u>

2. quick + –ly = _____

3. dangerous + –ly = _____

4. truthful + –ly = _____

5. glad + –ly = _____

6. mad + –ly = _____

7. delicate + –ly = _____

8. stern + –ly = _____

9. firm + –ly = _____

10. honest + –ly = _____

Sentence building

Make your own sentences with '**–ly**' adverbs.
Choose an action from Box A. Choose an adverb
from Box B. Use them together to build your own sentence.

Box A: actions	
reading	swimming
playing	running
climbing	singing
writing	chatting

Box B: –ly adverbs	
secretly	rudely
badly	quietly
sternly	delicately
dangerously	gladly

1. _____

2. _____

3. _____

4. _____

5. _____

6. _____

7. _____

8. _____

Comparative sentences

Fill in the gaps in each sentence. One has been done for you.

1. Annie's sunflower is tall, Emma's sunflower is <u>taller</u>_____ but Beth's sunflower is <u>the tallest</u>_____.

2. Zain can run fast, Harry runs _____ but Peter runs _____.

3. A torch is bright, the lamp is _____ but the sun is _____.

4. The afternoons are cold, the mornings are _____ but the nights are _____.

5. Your grandpa is old, mine is _____ but Rav's is _____.

6. This mouse is small, this bee is _____ but this ant is _____.

7. This blanket is soft, your jumper is _____ but my scarf is _____.

8. My baby brother is loud, my older brother is _____ but I am _____!

Comparisons quiz

Answer these questions about the people around you.

1. Who is the tallest? _____

2. Who is the youngest? _____

3. Who is the oldest? _____

4. Who is the loudest? _____

5. Who is the fastest? _____

6. Who is the smallest? _____

7. Who is the kindest? _____

8. Who is the calmest? _____

Now write three of your own sentences using **–est** words.

_____

_____

_____

_____

_____

_____

Building coordinating conjunction sentences

Cut out the sentence parts and the coordinating conjunctions. Match them together to build longer sentences that use coordinating conjunctions and stick them down.

and	or	but
I got new boots.	We could go to the park	I like toast for breakfast
you can choose ice cream.	I got a new coat	it has been sunny all day.
I tidied my room.	I finished my homework	You can choose an ice lolly
I like eggs more than toast.	we could go to the shops.	They said it would rain
but	or	and

Finishing coordinating conjunction sentences

Finish each sentence by adding a coordinating conjunction and then making up the rest of the sentence.

Remember that the second part of the sentence should make sense on its own and don't forget the full stop.

Coordinating conjunctions
and   but   or

1. Today was very sunny _____

_____

2. Kelly loves eating apples _____

_____

3. I might go to bed early _____

_____

4. Laura went to a party _____

_____

5. Roger got a pet rabbit _____

_____

6. Carl plays cricket _____

_____

7. We could go to the library _____

_____

8. Saturday is my favourite day _____

Finding subordinating conjunctions

Find and draw a circle around the subordinating conjunctions **because**, **if**, **when** and **that**.
Underline the first and second parts of each sentence using different colours.

1. I love my birthday because I have a party.

2. You might get hot if you keep your jumper on all day.

3. I always cry when I watch a sad film.

4. I told my dad that I would be home by six o'clock.

5. I am at after-school club because Dad is running late.

6. I am excited that it is snowing.

7. We woke up when the birds started singing.

8. I eat toast for breakfast because I'm not keen on cereal.

Subordinating conjunction sentences

Choose the best subordinating conjunction to complete each sentence

Subordinating conjunctions

because	if
when	that

1. It is coldest in England _____ it is winter.

2. I said _____ Jamal could come to my house for tea.

3. I can play at Jessie's house next week _____ I get all my homework finished first.

4. My grandad is gardening _____ he enjoys it.

5. Our teacher told us _____ we are going to visit the museum.

6. We could practise our play _____ we have finished our writing.

7. I was reading a book _____ I had some spare time.

8. India told us _____ she is going on holiday.

Challenge

Write your own sentences using the subordinating conjunctions.

_____

_____

_____

_____

Finding nouns

Find and circle the noun that is being described.

1. The magnificent, green, scaly dragon soared across the sky.

2. Nan tipped the delicate china teapot with the chipped spout.

3. The busy supermarket on the corner was about to close.

4. The fragrant vegetable curry is in the oven.

5. A smart brown envelope arrived in the post.

6. My old black biro pen is drying up.

7. Her adorable baby was falling asleep.

8. He gulped the crisp sweet apple juice.

Expand these nouns yourself to describe them.

T-shirt   book   car

_____

_____

_____

Building expanded noun phrases

Build expanded noun phrases by choosing a noun from the first box then choosing words and phrases to describe your noun from the second box.

You can also add your own descriptions, if you want. Write them on the lines underneath. Will your descriptions be silly or sensible?

Nouns
phone   rabbit   fish   boy   girl
pen   van   bike   tent   house

Descriptive words and phrases
red   pink   yellow   fluffy   sharp   gloopy
sad   happy   grumpy   broken   refreshing   rainy
woolly   old   with the long tail   with the curly hair

_____

_____

_____

_____

_____

_____

_____

Ice-cream noun phrases

Design an ice-cream stall with as many different flavours, toppings and sizes as you can think of.
Ask your friends which ice cream they would like and tell them to be specific. Write down their three favourite combinations.

Noun phrases to specify

Be specific about each item below by writing a description to make it clear. One has been done for you.

1. Which shoes? _The white leather shoes with the green laces and black soles._

2. Which jumper? _____

_____

3. Which film? _____

_____

4. Which drink? _____

_____

5. Which game? _____

_____

6. Which party? _____

_____

7. Which car? _____

_____

8. Which book? _____

_____

9. Which friend? _____

_____

10. Which computer? _____

_____

Is it a statement?

Remember a statement is a sentence that tells us a fact.
Tick the statements below.

1. The old man walked up the hill. ☐

2. the small noisy dog ☐

3. Tuesday is the day before Wednesday. ☐

4. There were six cows grazing in the field. ☐

5. cup of tea with milk ☐

6. I need to get some bread from the shop. ☐

7. I wake up at seven o'clock every morning. ☐

8. rice and peas at dinner ☐

Writing statements

Explain what a statement is in your own words.

_____

_____

_____

Now, write statements about the following topics. Remember your capital letters and full stops.

1. swimming _____

2. plants _____

3. the weather _____

4. school _____

5. butterflies _____

6. friends _____

7. shopping _____

8. clothes _____

Question words

Which question word is missing from each question?

Use the words from the box to fill in the gaps. You can use each word more than once. Some questions will suit more than one question word.

why	what	where	how	who	when

1. _____ do birds eat?

2. _____ did you see at the park?

3. _____ time will you get there?

4. _____ is Dad coming home?

5. _____ are you feeling today?

6. _____ have you put my shoes?

7. _____ did you do that?

8. _____ would you like to play?

Questions

Read these questions and write your answers.

1. What is your name? _____

2. How old are you? _____

3. Who do you sit next to in class? _____

4. What is your favourite colour? _____

5. What is your favourite food? _____

Now write questions to match these answers.

1. _____

I wake up at 7 o'clock in the morning.

2. _____

My favourite game is I-Spy.

3. _____

I have one sister and one brother.

4. _____

My birthday is on June 4th.

5. _____

I help my mum by tidying my toys up.

Sorting exclamations

Sort the exclamations by writing them in the correct boxes.

- How wonderful!

- What a surprise!

- How very strange!

- What fun!

- Oh no, not again!

- Go away!

- How frightening!

- I am so cross with you!

Exclamations that show surprise	Exclamations that show anger
Exclamations that show happiness	Exclamations that show fear

Writing exclamations

Imagine you met a monster. Write all the things you would say and think. Which sentences need exclamation marks? Check to make sure you have added them. Then read your exclamations to a partner to show how you use your voice to read with shock, surprise, fear or excitement.

_____

_____

_____

_____

_____

_____

_____

_____

_____

_____

_____

Imperative verb search

Imperative verbs are sometimes called 'bossy' words because they tell someone to do something. Colour in all the boxes that contain imperative verbs.

eat	flower	fetch	friends	pack
blue	stop	dinner	cut	go
turn	penned	shoes	pleasing	talk
chop	fold	hairbrush	wait	listen
write	computer	colouring	matted	spooned
car	read	sleeping	change	draw

How many imperative verbs did you find? _____

Commands

Think of all the things you are asked to do each day by your family, your teacher and your friends. Write them as a list of commands. Start by thinking about when you wake up in the morning and finish with going to bed at night. Some have been done for you.

Wake up.

Get dressed.

Eat your breakfast.

Past or future tense

Read each sentence. Tick 'past' or 'future' to show whether the sentence describes something that has already happened or something that will happen. Then, find and underline all the verbs (action words).

	past	future
1. I swam across the pool.		
2. I will swim tomorrow.		
3. We walked to school this morning.		
4. I am going to walk to school on Friday.		
5. I must finish my homework tonight.		
6. I finished my homework on Sunday.		
7. I will open my present in the morning.		
8. I opened my present last night.		

Yesterday

Write a diary entry about what you did yesterday. Use verbs in the past tense from the word box to help you.

went	ate	played	walked	talked
wrote	counted	thought	said	

_____

_____

_____

_____

_____

_____

_____

_____

_____

Present tense verb search

Verbs in the present tense describe what is happening now. Colour in all the boxes that contain present tense verbs.

carrot	sticky	play	clever	chat
wash	try	nice	dance	trucks
iron	plums	runs	jumper	green
café	laughs	sink	bite	carries
shirt	cot	cries	window	yours
see	use	fingers	sleep	rides

How many present tense verbs did you find? _____

Past and present tense sentences

Write 'past' or 'present' next to each sentence to show which tense it is in.

1. I see the dolphins in the sea. _____

2. I sleep deeply all night. _____

3. I cried at the sad film. _____

4. I rode my bike to school. _____

5. I carry the bags for Mum. _____

6. I danced at the disco. _____

7. I play at Gran's house on Sundays. _____

8. I use a pen to write stories. _____

Sorting tenses

Sort the verbs into the correct columns to show if they are in the 'past progressive tense' or the 'present progressive tense'.

am eating	were cleaning	was melting	are relaxing
is riding	are digging	was singing	were making
was writing	was cutting	is reading	is sewing

Past progressive tense	Present progressive tense

The volcano

Write about life in a town that is near a volcano that has erupted.

Use the past progressive tense to write sentences describing what people were doing when the volcano erupted. Then use the present progressive tense to write sentences about what people are doing in the town now.

You can use your own ideas or use suggested words from the boxes to help you.

past progressive	present progressive
was **were**	**am** **is** **are**
watching waiting	cleaning celebrating
shopping playing	visiting hoping
working	building planting

_____

_____

_____

_____

_____

_____

_____

_____

Correcting sentences

Correct these sentences. Add capital letters at the beginning and anywhere else you think they are needed, and then add suitable end punctuation.

1. daisy and joe went on the bus to visit their nan in devon

2. the teachers found a lolly stuck to the head teacher's chair

3. the bird ate a worm and splashed in the bird bath

4. pascal met jeremy and then watched rovers fc play in the final

5. edwina was so hungry she thought she might faint

6. the hall was full of people who had come to listen to the talk

7. gemma ordered an english breakfast with all the extras

8. is verity really moving house tomorrow

Writing sentences

Write three correctly punctuated sentences about birds.

1. _____

2. _____

3. _____

Write three correctly punctuated sentences about a party.

1. _____

2. _____

3. _____

Write three correctly punctuated sentences about the beach.

1. _____

2. _____

3. _____

Adding commas to sentences

Add commas in the correct places in these sentences.

1. We saw sharks stingrays turtles crabs otters and jellyfish at the aquarium.

2. We bought carrots potatoes turnips cauliflower broccoli and cabbage at the supermarket.

3. I play with Maise Malika Joe Scott Tara and Dana at school.

4. I have my bed wardrobe drawers desk clothes TV and alarm clock in my room.

5. We planted daisies daffodils pansies tulips and roses in the garden.

6. I have pens pencils a ruler sharpener eraser and some stickers in my pencil case.

Making lists

Write a list of pets, things in your house, colours and people in your family. Include at least three items in each list. Use commas to separate the items in your lists but remember to use 'and' between the last two items, not a comma.

1. pets: _____

_____

2. in my house: _____

_____

3. colours: _____

_____

4. my family: _____

_____

Matching contractions to whole words

Cut out the words. Match the shortened word to the whole words.

she'll	can't	should not	we are
I am	was not	had not	he is
we've	we're	wasn't	didn't
shouldn't	they are	she will	we will
did not	hadn't	we have	they're
he's	can not	we'll	I'm

Writing contractions

Rewrite the abbreviated words as whole words.

Contractions	Whole words
she's	
aren't	
you're	
they're	
won't	
don't	
I'll	
wouldn't	
hasn't	

Rewrite the whole words as contractions.

Whole words	Contractions
did not	
he will	
he would	
it is	
is not	
I would	
they will	
what is	
who is	

Showing possession

Complete the final column in the table to show who owns what. Remember to use an apostrophe and an **s** each time.

Who owns it?	What do they own?	How do we write it?
Luke	shoes	**Luke's shoes**
Zahid	pen	
Maria	computer	
Sophie	ball	
Gregory	bag	
Nick	book	
Matt	hat	
Amy	scooter	

Using possessive apostrophes

Write a sentence about the things people own.
One has been done for you.

1. A toaster belonging to Sarah

Paul borrowed Sarah's toaster.

2. A car belonging to Mrs Jones

_____

3. Some slippers belonging to Mr Sanchez

_____

4. A calculator belonging to Chantelle

_____

5. A book belonging to Joshua

_____

6. A bike belonging to a friend

_____

7. Some nuts belonging to a squirrel

_____

8. A nest belonging to a bird

_____